WILD SWIMMING
THE RIVER WYE

BY ANGELA JONES

Hello

I am Angela Jones and for 54 years on this beautiful planet, I've lived a life without lanes.

The River Wye runs through my veins. I am fortunate to have experienced over 30 years of swimming, kayaking and wild camping this river, and appreciating its beauty and diversity. Sharing this joy over the last 13 years has been my constant companion, Jack - my rescue dog and co-adventurer.

I am known as the wild woman of the Wye because I can be found above and below its waters all year round. I'm often asked advice about wild swimming in the river so I have written this book to share my life-long passion.

I feel privileged that this is my office and my playground, and I am very protective of this magical gem. Every day the Wye continues to intrigue, surprise and delight. Getting to know it over the many years has been a fascinating journey.

I want to share my love and knowledge of this amazing river so you can respect it, enjoy it safely and improve your swim technique too. I hope to enhance your wild swimming adventures while preserving the river for generations to come. So, join me on this journey and swim the wondrous Wye!

Cover Image: Stuart Pearce

River Wye Source to Sea
250kms (155 miles)

NORTH

• PLYNLIMON

• RHAYADER

Wales / England Border

• WHITNEY-ON-WYE

• BUILTH WELLS

• HAY-ON-WYE

GLASBURY

HEREFORD •

HOLME LACY •

HOARWITHY •

• ROSS-ON-WYE

SYMONDS YAT •

• KERNE BRIDG

MONMOUTH •

• REDBROOK

• BROCKWEIR

CHEPSTOW •

River Severn

*Angela and Jack visit the source of the
River Wye in the Plynlimon Mountains*

Contents

Image: G. K. Wood

Leisure

What is this life if, full of care,
We have no time to stand and stare

No time to stand beneath the boughs,
And stare as long as sheep and cows

No time to see, when woods we pass,
Where squirrels hide their nuts in grass

No time to see, in broad daylight,
Streams full of stars, like skies at night

No time to turn at Beauty's glance,
And watch her feet, how they can dance

No time to wait till her mouth can
Enrich that smile her eyes began

A poor life this if, full of care,
We have no time to stand and stare

W H Davies
Local poet. Born 3 July 1871

A bit more about the author

Me? Well, I'm a rather feral person and a life-long wild swimmer.

My life has been full of spontaneity and adventure, with plenty of challenging aspects along the way, to say the least. I live in the moment, the here and now. My energy and enthusiasm for nature and the great outdoors ooze out of every pore of my weather-hardened skin. I do not over-analyse, I don't stress, I don't hold onto negatives - I just live the moment.

I was born in Greenford and moved several times before leaving home at 15. I grew up fast and tough. I remember a careers officer in school asking what I wanted to do when I left. I replied, "A life of adventure and exploring." Where or what, I didn't know.

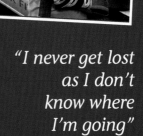

"I never get lost as I don't know where I'm going"

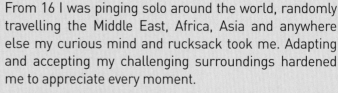

From 16 I was pinging solo around the world, randomly travelling the Middle East, Africa, Asia and anywhere else my curious mind and rucksack took me. Adapting and accepting my challenging surroundings hardened me to appreciate every moment.

The first time I stumbled across the Wye was in my late teens; I had just come back from travelling in the Middle East. Its beauty was breathtaking and the water invited me in. I didn't know what the river was called then, but the excitement I felt and the sheer beauty in front of me stopped me in my tracks.

I continued to bob around the world discovering, seeking, curiously embracing countries and cultures. But all through my travels and different episodes in life, the Wye always engulfed me with a feeling of belonging, I don't know why or how it had that effect and I've never over-analysed it, it just did. I knew after so much travelling, it was a place like no other in the world.

From the age of 32, for over 20 years, I unintentionally became an international athlete and even raced several times at senior world level and age group, doing a bit of mountain running, cross country, triathlon, swimming, duathlon, aquathon and cycling. I remember athletes and coaches would often say, "If you concentrated on one thing, you'd be unstoppable." Maybe I didn't want to be. Nature is my home, my training ground and my playground and it definitely enhances my soul.

My philosophy, which runs through my life, is to never take yourself too seriously - great things are achieved when you relax. A smile and enjoyment are in everything I do; I have always had the imagination and sense of adventure to make things fun and relaxed, and that's when habit takes hold.

I've played all over the world, swimming in different locations, from sub-zero temperatures at the tectonic plates in Iceland to crossing the wild lochs of Scotland. However, my heart still belongs to the Wye. I taste its sweetness, I feel its strengths, its moods, its solitude, its pain. The changing seasons, the increase in tourists, the migration of the birds, I watch it all from above and below the water.

I feel very protective of this beautiful landscape. I wrote this book to introduce others to the area and offer advice to enjoy wild swimming whilst respecting this magnificent part of the world.

Wild swimming is one of the fastest growing sports in Britain and is inclusive to all. Whether you want to enjoy a quick dip or distance, the River Wye offers it all. The well documented health benefits are vast and I share some of these with you on page 11.

Within this book you'll find important information on the Swimmer's Code of Conduct. Please take the time to read this so you can prepare yourself and enjoy your visit to the River Wye.

It is hugely important to respect the river. I have witnessed people throwing themselves in without any knowledge of the immense danger they are putting themselves in. There are undercurrents, rapids, hidden boulders and debris and the Wye is one of the fastest rising rivers at up to 30cm per hour. Weather conditions can exhaust swimmers and hypothermia can easily set in.

So, let's appreciate the Wye's diversity, understand the beauty and enjoy it safely while caring for the environment together.

Enjoy your swim and swim safely

Angela

"Open water swimming is one of the fastest growing sports in the UK and it's inclusive to all"

The old railway bridges at Monmouth

Image: I. McCallum

Image: M. Flight

The River Wye

The River Wye (or Afon Gwy as it is known in Welsh) is truly the most magical and wonderful river I've swum.

The Latin name for Wye is 'Vaga' meaning 'wandering'. The fifth longest river in the UK, the Wye meanders through the borders of England and Wales, running 155 miles (250kms) rising from its source in Plynlimon, mid Wales, high in the Cambrian Mountains where it then travels through a variety of places including Rhayader, Hay-on-Wye, Hereford (the only city on the River Wye), Ross-on-Wye, Monmouth and Chepstow, ending at the River Severn. In some places the River Wye defines the border between England and Wales.

Voted one of the nation's favourite rivers in 2010, the Wye runs through 58 miles (93kms) of a designated Area of Outstanding Natural Beauty (AONB) which offers it the same level of protection as a National Park. It has been granted a Special Site of Scientific Interest (SSSI) and given the status of a European Special Area of Conservation (SAC) under the European Habitats Directive. It is also regarded as one of the finest lowland landscapes in Britain.

*"If You Truly Love Nature,
You Will Find Beauty Everywhere."*

VINCENT VAN GOGH

Symonds Yat West

Image: J.Milne-Smith

Image: M. Flight

The benefits of cold water swimming

ANTI-INFLAMMATORY
One of the best known anti-inflammatory activities, effective for arthritis, circulation and injury recovery.

BOOSTS YOUR IMMUNE SYSTEM
Boosts white blood cell count and over time your body becomes better at activating its defences.

GIVES YOU A NATURAL HIGH
Activates Endorphins, the chemical the brain produces to make us feel good. Exercise has also been proven to treat depression.

REDUCES STRESS
Studies have identified the link between cold water and stress reduction.

IMPROVES YOUR CIRCULATION
Flushes your veins, arteries and capillaries, forcing blood to the surface and helping to warm your extremities.

Repeated exposure to cold water helps adapt us to the cold.

INCREASES YOUR LIBIDO
Boosts Oestrogen and Testosterone production, adding an edge to fertility and libido.

BURNS CALORIES
Because the heart has to pump faster and the body must work harder to keep everything warm.

POSITIVE EFFECT ON MENOPAUSE
Studies have proven the positive effects of cold water swimming and the menopause. It is hugely beneficial to improve general health and well-being.

SOCIALISE AND MAKE NEW FRIENDS
There's a great sense of community and camaraderie amongst cold water swimmers.

18-year-old Doreen Davey landed the largest salmon in the Wye in 1923 (59.5lbs)

Early memories of childhood on the Wye

Researching for the book, I spoke to locals about their memories of the river.

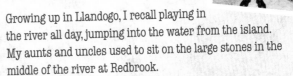

'Pogging' eels was a common activity; there were hundreds in the Wye during the summer months. We'd catch them by forking them, collect them in pillowcases and squeeze out the slime, then take them home to be cooked by Mum (always fried and sliced!).

Growing up in Llandogo, I recall playing in the river all day, jumping into the water from the island. My aunts and uncles used to sit on the large stones in the middle of the river at Redbrook.

In the 1950s we'd see lots of water voles plopping in and out of the water and salmon leaping. Howard Brown was a café owner in Llandogo, known for serving fresh Wye Salmon teas - we called him the Elver King.

A Canadian man, Mr Force, would pay a fortune to fly over especially to fish for salmon. We'd play alongside him all day and he was so polite, he never once told us off!

In 1963, the river froze solid and we used to ice skate across it. One boy sadly lost his life.

Glen Roderick, 71. Ex Mayor of Usk

Image: M. Flight

My father taught my sister and I to swim in the Wye; we grew up in Bredwardine, on the banks of the river.

I have early memories of sitting in the shallows, scooping up handfulls of elvers!

Summer childhood memories all involve the River Wye; gliding through the Water Crowfoot Weed and waking in the middle of the night, climbing out of my bedroom window, onto the roof and running down to the river for a night time dip. The river always drew me!

Kate, Bredwardine

I remember seeing salmon leaping 2 - 3 feet in the air from the water, and also wading into the Wye to rescue children from the elvers!

Guy Hemmington, Hampton Bishop

A sharp-eyed Cormorant

Image: P. Bennell

Wildlife and water of the Wye

Important for both nature conservation and recreation, the River Wye is an important conservation area and in all there are three Special Areas of Conservation (SAC), four National Nature Reserves (NNR) and over forty Sites of Special Scientific Interest (SSSI) in the Wye Valley Area of Natural Beauty (AONB). These help protect and preserve this essential habitat of native woodland, important wildlife habitats, limestone gorges and geology.

The Wye is one the best salmon fishing rivers in the UK and attracts many visitors each year. The Wye Valley Walk follows the river for much of its journey and there is a scenic viewpoint at the Biblins where the three counties of Monmouthshire, Herefordshire and Gloucestershire meet; this is known as Three Counties View.

Historically, the River Wye provided a crucial industrial gateway, linking towns along the river to import and export raw materials. Tourism was born in the Wye Valley in the 18th century, when people came to visit, in order to enjoy the beautiful river landscape. This is still a huge industry in the area, estimated to be worth over £100million annually.

Many businesses operate along the Wye. We have a duty of care to protect and put back, through respect and education for the livelihood that Nature has so graciously shared with us.

The huge richness and diversity of animals and plants that I encounter along the Wye is a treat like no other. Little Egrets are growing in numbers; the migrating Canada Geese and many other birds are an exciting sight to behold as spring emerges.

The joys of spending so much time in and under the water are that I become familiar with, and protective of the immense wildlife the Wye contains.

For the past 20 years Peregrine Falcons have nested in the limestone cliffs at Coldwell Rocks, Forest of Dean. From Symonds Yat Rock you can witness them hunting and raising their young between April and August.

Image: M. Cray

Image: M. Flight

Mandarin ducks

These beautiful, colourful birds are thought to have escaped from an exotic collection to make their home on some of our waterways, but they are really native to Japan, China and Russia. Nesting in tree holes above the ground allows them to frighten off any predators. They are quite shy but I have seen them along various stretches of the Wye.

Sand martins

Sand martins dig burrows into the sandy banks of the river. I look forward to their arrival from Africa every spring, and love watching them swoop across the surface of the water to catch insects. Look out for their nesting holes along the riverbanks, especially above beaches.

Image: P. Bennell

Swans and geese

Swans and geese are territorial animals. They are especially protective of their cygnets and, if they feel threatened, they can sometimes display aggressive behaviour. Do not enter or exit the water near a nest or an area where they are swimming. Respect their territory and pass quietly; I always take care and give them the utmost attention.

There is one section of the Wye where every year, in springtime, I see a lone white goose in the company of the migrating Canada Geese.

Image: I. Macdonald

Peregrine falcons

Whenever I swim past Symonds Yat Rock I slow down in the hope of seeing the peregrine falcons catching pigeons overhead. I've got to know the breeding pairs, and I recognise their screeches. There is no finer experience than to see the fledglings discovering their wings for the first time. The peregrine falcon is one of the fastest animals in the world and can reach speeds of 200mph when swooping down on prey, so it is thrilling to watch them in action.

Kingfisher

Image: Sarah H Hopwood

Cormorants

These large, dark-coloured birds are becoming a common sight along the river, perched on overhanging branches, drying their outstretched wings. Cormorants are superb at fishing, which sadly brings them into conflict with anglers, who sometimes persecute them.

Image: P. Bunnell

Dipper

I love these little chocolate brown birds with their distinctive white chest. They favour fast-flowing, shallow water and are most commonly seen near Wye tributaries dipping or bobbing up and down. They search under water for aquatic insects by stretching their wings against the current and pushing downwards to stay submerged.

Grey Heron

It's very easy to miss a heron, still as a statue, standing on the bank or in shallow water, eyeing up its prey. Sometimes, I hear their croaking and then spot them taking off into a slow, lazy flight, neck bent in an S-shape. Many of my swims are blessed by a sighting of this prehistoric-looking bird.

Kingfishers

Kingfishers appear to be increasing in number on the Wye. It's magical to watch them diving, or simply catch sight of an electric blue flash as they skim across the water. They are very territorial birds and will fiercely protect their area of the river; you can often see them circling their haunt.

Kingfishers nest in sandy riverbanks and primarily eat fish. However, they also enjoy tadpoles and freshwater shrimps. As they dive into the water to catch their prey, they close their eyes so they are actually fishing blind! When they are 25 days old the chicks are ready to leave the nest. The adults will feed them for four more days before driving them out to establish their own territory.

Image: Sarah H Hopwood

Image: **I. Macdonald**

Beaver

Beavers have been extinct in Britain for almost 500 years, but a small population has recently been introduced as part of a scheme to help prevent flash flooding on the Wye. They are natural engineers and it's hoped that their dams will slow the flow of water into the river. South Herefordshire and the Forest of Dean are the most likely places to come across a beaver; it will be a rare privilege if you see one.

Mink

You are more likely to see a mink than an otter, and they do look very similar, although the mink is a lot smaller. They have dark brown fur and a distinctive white chin and lower jaw.

Mink farms were established in the UK after the Second World War and, unfortunately, significant numbers escaped into the wild and became well established. They have become a dreadful threat to our native wildlife and are partly responsible for the declining population of water voles along the Wye.

Otter

Otters are elusive, but you might see their tracks along the mudbanks of the Wye. If they hear you coming, they will almost certainly take cover and can hold their breath underwater for up to 8 minutes at a time. They make their home and raise their pups in underground 'holts'. I've had the pleasure of watching a few over the years and recently witnessed a mother and two youngsters playing, seemingly oblivious to me while I was swimming.

Water voles

Once common, the water vole is Britain's fastest declining wild mammal, threatened by mink and habitat loss. They live in burrows on the riverbank and you can see signs that they are around if there is a 'lawn' of nibbled grass in front of the burrow with 45 degree cut ends. You can easily recognise their droppings because they are cigar-shaped.

The AONB has been involved in the 'Water Voles on the Wye' project, working to expand their range and numbers.

Water vole

Image: D. H. Read

Dragonfly

Dragonflies and Damselflies

These were some of the first insects to evolve almost 300 million years ago, earlier than the dinosaurs. Their huge eyes have thousands of lenses which gives them panoramic viewing and allows them to see their prey in any direction up to 12 metres away! It's quite difficult to tell the difference between them but a dragonfly is larger and keeps its wings open when it rests. You will see large clusters seeming to dance on the water's surface.

Damselfly   Image: I. Macdonald

Grass snakes and adders

They are a rare sight but can sometimes be spotted in or near the Wye. Grass snakes feed on frogs and fish, whereas adders prefer to hunt in dry areas. I have had the privilege to see both and it's always a treat because they are very shy, beautiful creatures. If you are lucky enough to see either, just stay calm, give them space and respect and they will do you no harm.

Adder   Image: I. Macdonald

Fish

The river Wye is a particularly unique habitat and is highly protected because it contains internationally important populations of salmon, twaite shad (a coastal fish that travels to the Wye to spawn in May), allis shad, eels, white-clawed crayfish, bullhead, chub, pike, trout, grayling, barbel and an array of other coarse species. The Wye is one of the UK's top rivers for barbel populations.

Some fish species appear particularly sensitive to disturbance, especially during the spawning seasons.

During winter, salmon spawn in the upper reaches of the Wye. Between 1st April and 31st July many coarse fish are breeding and twaite and allis shad use shallow gravel beds for egg laying.

Please do not disturb gravel beds at all times.

Salmon

The Wye is famous for its salmon, which swim thousands of miles across the Atlantic to spawn in the river each year. The largest ever caught in the Wye weighed 27kg (59.5lbs) and was landed by 18-year old Doreen Davey in 1923. Salmon can live in salt and fresh water: in the spring, those that survive will swim back downstream to the sea.

Lamprey

Similar in shape to the eel, there are three species of lamprey found in the Wye; they can grow up to 120cms (47ins) in length. In May and June lampreys migrate from the sea to the Wye to spawn.

Eels

The journey an elver (a baby eel) takes to reach the Wye is immense. It starts life as an egg in the Sargasso Sea, near Bermuda. Once the egg hatches and becomes larvae it drifts in the tide before hatching and swimming to Europe, a journey that can take 3 years. When they get close to the coast of Europe they become transparent and begin travelling upstream into rivers. Once in fresh water they change into elvers, then they grow larger, changing to a light yellow / brown colour. They can stay like that for many years until, at a certain point, becoming a 'silver' eel and starting the return journey to the Sargasso Sea and beginning the life cycle all over again.

Eels can live out of water for up to 12 hours as long as they remain in a damp environment and I have seen them crossing ponds and wetlands to reach the sea.

I am fascinated by eels but saddened to say I don't encounter as many as I used to when swimming underwater. Commercial fishing for elvers is common as they are exported to Japan where they are an expensive delicacy. The Rivers Wye and Severn are two of the largest elver fisheries in Europe.

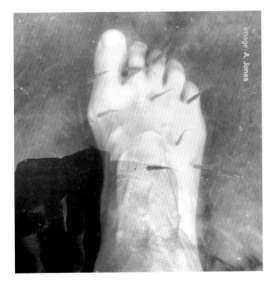

Image: A. Jones

Minnows

Small freshwater fish, minnows can be found in the River Wye all year round. They feed on insect larvae, plant debris and fish eggs, and I see them dancing around the water's edge at night when I camp along the river, glistening in the moonlight. They will give you a great pedicure - and it's free!

Himalayan Balsam

Identified easily by its distinctive pink flowers, this plant blooms between June and October and can be seen in drifts all along the Wye riverbanks. It has become a real nuisance because it prevents native species from growing, which is leading to habitat loss.

Nettles

'Stinging nettles' are a hugely important food source for wildlife, including frogs and toads. An ancient plant, widely used in herbal medicines, nettles are full of A, C and some B vitamins and contain calcium, potassium and iron. I love foraging for them and always toast some as a healthy snack when wild camping.

Woodland and riverside trees

In the Wye Valley almost 30% of the land is ancient woodland that provides rich habitats for wildlife, especially for rare species such as greater and lesser horseshoe bats.

A chain of ancient woodland, full of grand old trees and woodland flowers, stretches from Chepstow to Ross-on-Wye.

The magnificent trees growing along and overhanging the river are mainly species of willow and alder. Sadly, many of the banks are gradually eroding, which loosens the roots and leads to trees falling into the water. This can create unseen hazards for swimmers and additional dangers when the river floods, with trees and branches being swept downstream to lodge against bridges.

Water Crowfoot Weed

In the summer, this beautiful plant used to form extensive mats over large sections of the Wye, but pollution and green algae is starving it to the extent of serious decline. Water Crowfoot is a member of the buttercup family, that in June and July produces small white flowers. It needs fast-flowing water, with a stony bed, and its presence indicates the cleanliness of the water. The stem can be up to 20 feet long, which can be an entanglement hazard to swimmers, so relaxing and gliding over dense sections is advised. It is now protected and it is illegal to remove it.

Wild Garlic (Ramsons)

Wild garlic coats the floors of shaded wooded areas in spring and provides another clear sign of ancient woodland. It has been used in medicines as an ingredient to treat high cholesterol. The distinctive scent is divine and it always provides a tasty treat – milder and sweeter than the garlic we traditionally use in our kitchens. I love picking and eating a bit on my stroll through the woods - it's a Spring delicacy.

Wild Delights of the Wye

1. Goshawk family 2.. Little Egret 3. Barn Owl   4. Mallard Ducks   5. Goosanders   6 . Kingfisher 7. Flycatcher
8. Mandarin Duck   All images by local photographers

Early sunrise over the Wye, towards Lydbrook

Image: **M. Cray**

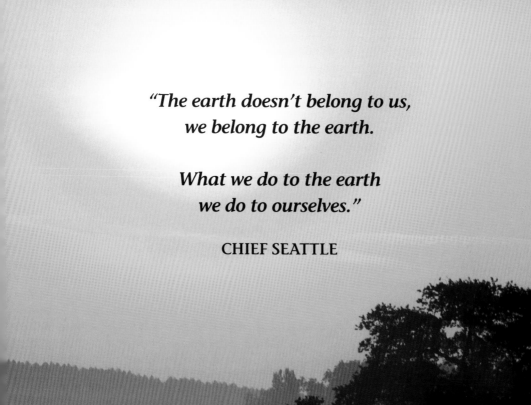

*"The earth doesn't belong to us,
we belong to the earth.*

*What we do to the earth
we do to ourselves."*

CHIEF SEATTLE

"Water safety is top of my list for every swimmer I take out regardless of age, as to have knowledge and respect for open water is paramount."

Family Swimming

In a world with an increasing reliance on technology the River Wye provides us with the perfect antidote to escape back to the peace and beauty of Nature.

Share the riverside with your family. Everyone can gain so much from spending time outside, especially children, who love to explore wild places. Helping your children engage with the natural world will form a lifelong respect for the great outdoors and our wildlife. A paddle or a dip can be a great family adventure!

Whenever I meet clients, they recall their memories of childhood, so use this as a great opportunity to build cherished childhood memories for your children.

Child Safe on the Wye and beyond

Wild swimming water safety for parents with children

Wild swimming is great fun. However, just as children need to be taught road safety, they also need education to stay safe in open water.

Children are naturally drawn to water, but they often don't see dangers. The Wye is a dangerous river and has taken many a child's life over the years. Children should be kept in sight at all times.

The following advice is given so you can help your children avoid the risks that wild swimming the Wye can pose and be kept safe whilst having fun in the water.

Even the best of swimmers are not drown-proof. Children who cannot swim well should always wear a buoyancy vest. All children, whatever ability, should be within arm's reach of a responsible adult at all times. The Wye has exceptionally strong currents above and below the surface making it impossible in places to fight against. The many memorials along the way are a stark reminder.

"I've had the great pleasure of working with some wonderful small people over the decades"

Keep a close eye on your children

In all aspects of life parental example is crucial in teaching life's lessons. Wild swimming is good for children but the example adults set and things we do will always stick with children.

- Always stay to well used, public sections of the Wye that you know are safe and shallow
- NEVER jump in! The shock of cold water can kill. Always get in slowly and acclimatise
- The not knowing what is below can permanently injure your child as the river bed is forever changing and branches and boulders have caught many out
- Stay away from weedy sections that are an easy entrapment
- Stay clear of fast-flowing sections and rapids
- Beware of your children getting cold. Wearing a wetsuit and a swim cap will help them retain heat
- Be aware of and look for the signs of hypothermia, which can be life threatening. It affects children if their body temperature drops below 35°C and signs include cold skin, tiredness, fast breathing, continuous shivering, confusion and changes in behaviour

Your choice!

Anyone who decides to swim in open water should remember that this, like other activities, is not entirely without risk.

Be safe. The most precious gift is a child.

Image: V. Willis

The River Wye Family Dips and Beaches

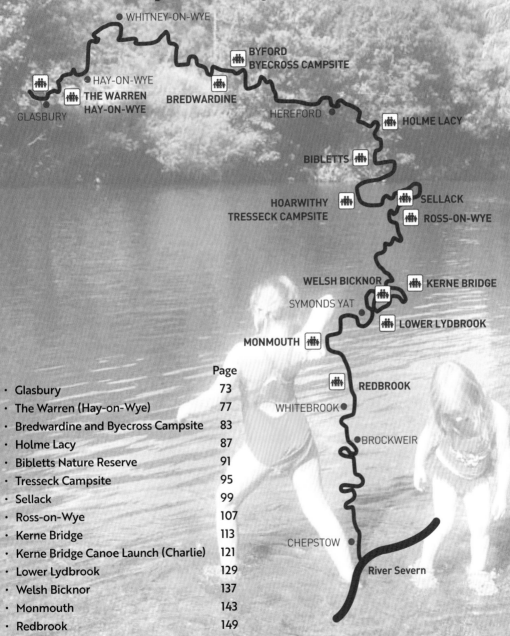

WHITNEY-ON-WYE

BYFORD
BYECROSS CAMPSITE

HAY-ON-WYE

THE WARREN
HAY-ON-WYE

BREDWARDINE

GLASBURY

HEREFORD

HOLME LACY

BIBLETTS

HOARWITHY
TRESSECK CAMPSITE

SELLACK

ROSS-ON-WYE

WELSH BICKNOR

KERNE BRIDGE

SYMONDS YAT

LOWER LYDBROOK

MONMOUTH

REDBROOK

WHITEBROOK

BROCKWEIR

CHEPSTOW

River Severn

Overall length 100 miles (160kms)

Swimmer's Code of Conduct

The swimmer's code of conduct offers advice to help protect you, your surroundings and others when you swim. Let's all follow the code to protect our wild swim passion, while working with others to share this beautiful, natural resource.

1. Consideration for Others

Be considerate of other people and help keep the countryside an enjoyable environment for us all:

- Respect local residents
- Avoid any conflict
- Park sensibly and don't cause obstructions by blocking gateways
- Keep noise to a minimum
- Come to shore at recognised landing places
- Be considerate of others when changing
- Do not trespass private property or moorings

Be fishing friendly

- Pass anglers quietly to keep noise and disturbance to a minimum
- Keep away from banks being fished
- Follow reasonable directional requests
- Look out for fishing lines as hooks can easily get embedded!
- Sometimes this is not always reciprocated - I have been casted at during occasional swims. But I will always endeavour to pursue courtesy and respect for my fellow river users.

We must share the river and its enjoyment with others! Please do so responsibly.

Chris Brain, lifelong responsible fisherman

2. Personal Safety

You are responsible for your own safety and for others in your care.

Conditions on the Wye can change rapidly so I advise you check the river level prior to your swim.

You can do this via the Natural Resources Wales website **www.naturalresourceswales.gov.uk.**

Alternatively, you can check this with the Wye and Usk Foundation who provide free river level information on their website **www.wyeuskfoundation.org/conditions**

The Wye can be dangerous and has been the cause of many misadventures. It is at its most dangerous when there are strong currents, high water levels or cold weather conditions. Don't take risks and never underestimate the power of the river. The Wye is a fast flooding river, which can rise after heavy rain at a rate of over 30cm an hour.

Water Safety Code
Be aware of and follow the water safety code at all times:
1. Spot the dangers
Look out for potential dangers in and around the water
2. Take safety advice
Take advice from signs, weather reports and river agencies on levels

3. Don't go alone
- Never swim alone. Always let someone know your route
- Discuss emergency plans and knowledge of the route before you set off

- Groups/novice swimmers should be led by a suitably qualified open water instructor with local knowledge, First Aid qualifications and insurance
- Continue to support each other when you exit the water

You are only as strong as your weakest swimmer. Make sure you find out abilities before you venture on a wild swim. Discuss your early exit plans and ensure you all have safety kit and fully charged mobile phones in your tow floats.

4. Learn how to help
- In an emergency, call **999 / 112**

5. Be seen
- The Wye is a navigational river with some exceptionally busy stretches. Pay particular attention around rowing clubs (Ross-on-Wye and Monmouth) where the rowers are not facing forward and may not see you
- Wear a brightly coloured hat
- Swim with a tow float
- Always pass (port to port) so left of swimmers, boats etc.

6. Look after your environment
Protect the environment in and out of the water and do not leave anything behind except your footprints.

Care for Wildlife
- Avoid disturbing nesting birds along the riverbanks, particularly in spring
- Avoid damaging beds of waterweed

Image:G K Wood

- Stop activity if you are clearly disturbing any wildlife
- Leave the water immediately if requested by an Environment Agency Officer
- The river habitat and many species are protected by law, ignoring advice could result in enforcement action
- ALWAYS wash your wetsuit after use so cross contamination of water does not harm the ecology of this highly protected river
- Please do not make fires in the SAC or SSSIs as it is illegal and harms wildlife
- Please take all litter home with you

As wild swimmers we are all privileged guests in the Wye and should share the responsibility of protecting and respecting the wildlife and environment.

80% of swimmers are worried about what is in the water. I feel totally privileged every time I spot wildlife - fish, otters, the occasional seal or dolphin (both of which have been spotted in recent years below Bigsweir at the lower tidal section), kingfishers diving and eels enjoying the water crowfoot weed.

7. Conditions

As part of your safety you need to be aware of local conditions that could have an effect on your swim, such as adverse weather. For example:

- Any conditions that impact visibility, for example mist, fog or heavy, driving rain
- Lightning
- Strong winds that can create waves and easily exhaust swimmers
- Flood waters – the River Wye is a fast flooding river which can rise after heavy rain at a rate of 30cm an hour
- Snow or ice

The Wye can be dangerous in strong winds and easily exhaust swimmers!

The ever-changing Wye

2020 has seen the worst flooding ever recorded on the Wye, bursting its banks and causing erosion, damage and leaving much debris. In many places it has redesigned some sections of the Wye. This has been followed by a spring drought, with us experiencing the driest and warmest spring on record.

Water Temperature

In the UK the water will be cold at the start of the season (April / May) and will gradually warm up as the summer progresses. Inland waters tend to remain colder compared to the sea, and the temperature at the surface may appear warm but will be much colder beneath the surface.

In the Wye we have many deep sections of water and adjoining rivers and brooks that add an extra chill to some sections. To use a thermometer on surface water, gives an inaccurate reading and can be deceiving.

River Temperature			
MONTH	NORMAL	WARMEST	COLDEST
January	3.6°C	6.3°C	1.0°C
February	3.8°C	6.7°C	0.9°C
March	5.9°C	9.4°C	2.5°C
April	7.9°C	11.8°C	3.9°C
May	11.2°C	15.7°C	6.6°C
June	14.0°C	18.4°C	9.5°C
July	16.4°C	21.1°C	11.8°C
August	16.2°C	20.8°C	11.6°C
September	13.5°C	17.5°C	9.5°C
October	10.0°C	13.4°C	6.7°C
November	6.2°C	9.2°C	3.5°C
December	4.5°C	7.1°C	1.9°C

5. Navigation rights and access

Seek permission to enter and exit the river on private land. The Wye has been used for navigation for many years, as an important commercial waterway. Today you will mainly see canoes, kayaks, SUPs and rowing boats, except at Symonds Yat where passenger sightseeing boats are operating.

A public right of navigation extends from the Severn upstream to Hay Town Bridge on the main River Wye and on the River Lugg between its confluence with the Wye and Presteigne Town Bridge. Public navigation of the river upstream of Bigsweir Bridge is the responsibility of the Environment Agency.

Below Bigsweir Bridge, public right of navigation is under the Gloucester Harbour Trustees. The river is also tidal for this lower stretch and too dangerous to swim.

The right of navigation does not give a right of access to the riverbank other than at accepted public sites. You must seek permission from the landowner before entering and exiting your swim. Permission is also needed to camp or picnic on the banks of neighbouring fields.

Open water swimming is one the fastest growing sports in the UK and we need to make ourselves aware of the guidelines and risks of the wondrous Wye in order to have a safe and happy swim!

*"My senses have become acute to the Wye over the years:
I taste its sweetness and its pollutants.
Remember, we share the water - this is not a swimming pool."*

Image: M.Flight

Muddy, slippy, boggy mud is part of wild swimming the Wye

Cattle share the Wye. I recommend head up and mouth out on these sections!

Health Advice for Open Water Swimming the Wye and beyond

Even though the Wye is one of Britain's best loved rivers heed the advice to minimise any risk to your health.

The water quality of the Wye is generally good, but it does contain natural bacteria and other micro-organisms. Although the risk of contracting illness is small, there are sensible precautions which can help you to stay healthy:

- Do not swallow river water

- Cover cuts or sores with gloves or waterproof plasters

- Where possible, wash or shower after all swims

- Always wash your hands before eating

- Never swim after heavy rain, due to 'chemical run- off' from fields

- See your doctor if you feel ill after exposure to the water

If you develop flu-like symptoms it is possible you may have contracted Leptospirosis (also known as Weil's, a rare disease, but one which can have serious complications).

There are certain sections I avoid due to higher pollution, for example: sewage outlets, heavily farmed areas, under heavy traffic bridges, moored boats.

Next Hour 04:55 21:34

30°
0%
7

Sunny and
light winds

*Swim down from Biblins Bridge
to Monmouth*

Image : S.Pearce

42

Heat Stroke

When swimming for long periods of time and longer distance in warmer water, swimmers will lose fluids and can easily become dehydrated and / or suffer with heat stroke.

Heat stroke occurs when the core body temperature reaches high levels over 40°C.

Possible signs of heat stroke include:
- Dizziness, fainting, confusion
- Headache
- Lowered levels of response
- Nausea, vomiting
- Flushed, hot, dry skin

On hot days the reflection of the water can over cook our bodies, believe it or not, and lead to heat stroke!

If you are an experienced open water swimmer on a long swim you need to take on fluid and refuel for energy. I stop and refuel regularly as I know my energy levels will be depleted. I always swim with a tow float containing my kit. Not only am I being seen but I have the essentials with me, such as fuel, phone and spare kit.

Image: M. Flight

Hypothermia

People underestimate hypothermia and this is one of the biggest challenges I have with swimmers.

Hypothermia occurs when the core body temperature drops below 35°C (normal core body temperature is 37°C) Hypothermia may develop as a result of prolonged periods in cold open water. In turn, that leads to continued heat loss and it can even occur following a short dip if you are a novice.

In the water the body can lose approximately 20 to 30 times more heat than at the same temperature on land.

As a swimmer leaves the cold water their body temperature will continue to drop. It is vital that you monitor yourself and your swim buddies post swimming and that you are aware of the signs of deterioration:

- Can the swimmer dress themselves?
- Can the swimmer answer questions?
- Is the swimmer's speech deteriorating?

A casualty must be warmed up gradually, so the core body temperature is raised.

It is essential to get changed quickly when you have finished your swim! So many people don't do this and cold can kill. Swimmers are inclined to stand around chatting, their endorphins high, and that Eureka moment will distract from the essential mantra 'costume off, kit on!' This is why I always use a head thermometer to

show swimmers the real temperature their body has plummeted to! Warm clothes and movement are essential to bring your body temperature up and avoid putting the heart under unnecessary stress.

Wild swimming should complement our health, not put our health under stress. This is why it is so important to do it safely.

Cold Water Shock

In the UK all waters are cold enough to induce the effects of cold water shock, even in high summer. When entering cold water you often take a large breath without exhaling. You need to enter the water slowly, exhale and relax and control your breathing. This acclimatisation helps you focus your body and mind appropriately.

The first minute in the water is crucial – stay calm, relax and control your breathing.

When immersing in cold water a swimmer can go into cold water shock, which is the main cause of drownings. I do not advise jumping straight in as this can increase the chances of cold water shock.

Don't be dim, don't jump in!

Anything below 15°C is defined as cold water

Possible signs of cold water shock include:
• Breath holding
• Pale skin
• Hyperventilation
• Slowing of body functions and speech

Raynaud's Syndrome

Raynaud's Syndrome is a common condition which affects the blood supply to certain parts of the body, normally the fingers and toes, and is usually triggered by cold temperatures. Other parts of the body that can be affected include the ears, nose, nipples and lips.

Possible signs of Raynaud's include:
• Affected areas change colour to white, then blue and then red, as the blood flow returns
• Numbness, pain, and pins and needles
• Symptoms can last from a few minutes to several hours.

I have had several swimmers who are affected by this and that is why it is essential to know your own body and to let others know any conditions that might impact your swim. It should not stop you from swimming but will affect your kit and warm up routine, and also extra help you may want from swim buddies.

Recommended Equipment for the Wye

Wetsuits

I use wetsuits on my longer guided swims with clients and recommend using one for your own comfort and safety. Not only are they good at retaining body temperature and providing a level of buoyancy, but they also protect your skin from boulders and rocks that you may come across along many sections of the Wye.

Wetsuits don't have to cost a fortune but they must fit and do the job! I have seen so many people buy ill-fitting ones that hinder their swimming. I personally use ORCA or the new Michael Phelps range, which I find perfect for what I do.

ALWAYS wash your wetsuit after use to avoid cross contamination of water

Tow Floats

Tow floats are a device which make you more visible in the water. They also offer a welcomed amount of buoyancy should you need a rest! Tow floats are inflatable, brightly coloured packs which are tethered around your waist while swimming. They can also be used to carry personal belongings such as emergency kit and a phone. They are ideal for swimming the Wye as you can swim downstream, put your kit on when you reach your destination, then walk or run back.

I recommend the 30-litre rucksack tow float by Swim Secure, endorsed by RLSS.

Goggles

Goggles are primarily for keeping water out of your eyes when swimming. Make sure your goggles have an anti-fog coating because a hot face and cold water can steam up goggles and hinder sighting, which is crucial when open water swimming.

If your goggles continue to mist up, rinse them at home in baby shampoo to help clear the insides.

I recommend Aqua Sphere Seal goggles; they are lightweight, have UVA/UVB protection and are like a small scuba mask. They are so comfortable and have a wider field of vision, which makes them ideal for the river terrain.

Swim Caps

Swim caps reduce heat loss and help maintain your core temperature. They also enhance your visibility to other water users so choose a brightly coloured one to make sure you stand out – be bold and be seen!

Too much hair conditioner will make your hat slip off!

I wear two hats in the winter, so under my usual silicone swim cap I will always wear a neoprene one that fastens under my chin and covers my ears as it's crucial to keep your head warm and hair out of your eyes.

Water Shoes

These are a must as the Wye has many shallow, stony sections. Swimming with suitable water shoes allows you easy access out of the water at any time as you have suitable grips to aid your exit along a bank. Water shoes can also protect you against hidden dangers, such as fish hooks or glass.

3 questions I am always asked by other water users:

1. How far are you going?

2. Is it cold?

3. Why?

Be prepared, you're highly likely to be asked the same things!

Winter kit

My recommendation on kit that does the job!

As I live in the water all year round, I'm always being asked to test out kit.

With so much inferior product on the market it's a difficult task for most people to know what's what: this is my individual preference.

My Crewsaver drysuit fleece is the best bit of kit I've EVER bought for wild swimming. It allows you to dress quickly, straight after any swim and however cold you are. It takes seconds merely to get the wet costume off and pull this on (no underwear needed), just instant warmth; and compact enough to put in your tow float, allowing you to exit anywhere.

I always use a folding stand mat to keep my feet off the ground and warm. This prevents dragging dirt through your clothes as you dress.

For hands, the Orca 3m neoprene long sleeve glove is my favourite if I'm going a distance in winter.

On my feet, C-skins 3m are really the best winter socks I've worn; long-lasting and enabling movement in the toes.

Water shoes need a good strong sole that allows safe walking, entry and exit on slippery, stony surfaces, as well as providing protection from hitting large rocks - a must on the Wye. Flimsy ones will not stop you from slipping or protect you from fishhooks, sharp debris or even glass. I can't over-emphasise the importance of these all year round for the Wye. (*photo at bottom of the page*)

As the temperatures drop even lower, my Charlie McLeod Eco Robe comes out. That does the job!

Remember all kit needs to be washed and dried thoroughly to stop cross contamination of different water sources as invasive spices can last up to 14 days on damp kit.

Please take winter swimming seriously as hypothermia kills: acclimatisation skills and reading open water takes years of learning.

It's not a competition to see how long you can stay in or how little you wear. Cold water swimming should complement health not put our body under stress; that's why I always take my clients' temperatures before they go into water and won't let them leave till it's back to normal.

Cheap shoes that a fishhook has gone through.

Enjoy but be safe x

Your kit can be a killer!!

Could YOU be cross contaminating our waters?

Regrettably, the increasing number of people entering the Wye and beyond to improve their own health is seriously compromising the health of the river itself.

And few are aware of it.

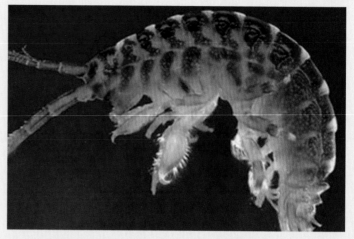

For example, equipment and clothing that has NOT been thoroughly dried or sterilised can carry and spread invasive species and diseases with devastating affects. Of course, this applies to all water users, including canoeists, paddle boarders, kayakers and fishermen/women).

Serious threats to the health of the river include **Crayfish Plague, Killer Shrimp** and **Gyrodactylus Salaris(GS)**.

It is essential that we take precautions to stop this disaster developing as these invasive species can live up to 14 days in damp wetsuits and other swim gear.

The **Killer Shrimp** is a recent threat from Eastern Europe and has established itself within Cardiff Bay and several other sites across the UK.

The **North American Signal Crayfish** is a fungal plague which is carried on equipment and clothing that has been in contact with infected water and/or crayfish.

Gyrodactylus Salaris (GS) is yet another potentially damaging plague, which affects salmon and can be brought in from the continent. It has already caused devastation in Norwegian rivers.

What you must do as a Responsible Water User

If you intend to reuse your equipment and clothing ie: wetsuits, tow floats, goggles, hats, gloves, water shoes, swimming costumes, etc, on trips to a variety of waters in the UK, or abroad, and there is less than 7 days between exiting and entering the different waters, you MUST ensure that clothing and equipment has been properly STERILISED by any one of the following methods:

A: Drying to a minimum of 20 degrees C for at least 2 days.

B: Heating to above 60 degrees C for at least one hour.

C: Deep freezing for at least 24 hours.

D: Immersion of materials in a solution of concentration indicated for a minimum of 10 minutes.

Virkon 1%

Wescodyne1%

Sodium hydroxide 0.2%

3% sodium chloride (common salt)

There are no known wetsuit cleaning products that protect the river from these invasive species. Many cleaning products contain phosphates (which stimulate excessive algae growth), EDTA, chlorine, enzymes or chemical plasticisers.

Nature – and in this case, the rivers – has been, and continues to be, incredibly supportive to our mental and physical health. Please let us return that compliment and take care of their health too.

BEFORE IT'S TOO LATE - DON'T CROSS CONTAMINATE.

Image: G. K. Wood

The woeful demise of our wonderful Wye

I have been witnessing and monitoring closely over the past decades - and particularly the last five years - the increase in farming pollution, slurry discharge, water extraction for irrigating farm fields, contamination from chemical crop sprays and industries, and even contamination from raw sewage entering our river.

I've also witnessed a huge increase in plastic in our Wye, which comes from businesses, tourists and locals, and it is pitiful to see it clogging up the river.

There are many people who care for the Wye but alas, too many who take, without a thought for the effect on this treasured gem, whose veins support the ecological biodiversity to so many species.

Over the past three or four years I have witnessed an increase in green algae.

There are now serious concerns over the permanently damaging effects these severe blooms are having on the ecology of this highly protected river. The proportion of phosphate in the Wye from agriculture has doubled in the past six years. The upper river in Wales is now a significant source, following a large expansion of the poultry industry over the last decade. Since 2008, the catchment of one of the river's tributaries in Powys now

On a mission to save the Wye: Angela 'greened up' for a Press article to highlight the growing problem of algae.

hosts an extra ten million chickens. This has produced massive amounts of highly reactive phosphates from their manures.

The river is now failing its permitted levels of phosphate under the EU Habitats Directive. This is very worrying.

I utilise my media profile as a springboard to bring awareness to this disaster, which is unfolding in front of our very eyes. I dedicate my time with local ecologists and agencies, and have worked with my MP supporting Greenpeace to heighten awareness and bring a Bill to Parliament to clean up our rivers. I was also asked to take part in a BBC Panorama programme and use my first-hand knowledge of raw sewage in our rivers.

I am not a loan crusader or a crank. I just know what's right - and what's not - and the colossal importance of preserving the health of the water and the wildlife of the Wye and beyond, for generations to come.

Why oh why pollute the Wye?

HOW CAN YOU HELP?

In Wales you can contact Natural Resources Wales, add the email subject as 'FAO CEO, RE: Demise of the River Wye' Email to: **enquiries@naturalresourceswales.gov.uk**

In England, you can contact Natural England **enquiries@naturalengland.org.uk**

The Environment Agency: **enquiries@environment-agency.gov.uk** And also your local MPs.

Swim Tips

I have been a swim teacher, international athlete and an open water swim specialist over the last three decades. I am sharing my techniques with you so you can use them to enjoy the open water safely, whatever your ability!

Acclimatisation and Overcoming Panic
Acclimatisation is a key part of the pre-swim routine that can help prevent panic on entering the water. It also helps to get the body used to the cold water.

Understand the river. It's not about conquering miles, it's about working with the environment you're in. Reading the river will ensure you get the best out of your swim and your day.

The river will always be a dangerous environment that demands respect and forward planning. It's forever changing, and complacency can lead to injury, even fatality, of which too much is occurring on the Wye and beyond!

Wild swimming is the fastest growing sport in Britain. Done right, it's amazing, but done wrong it can be treacherous.

Mental attitude
Open water swimming is all about relaxing to focus your body and mind. Detach from the cold water by having positive thoughts and never saying negative phrases such as 'it's cold'. Concentrate on controlling your breathing by slowly breathing in for 3 and out for 6; look around, take in the beauty of your surroundings, and tell yourself how privileged you are to share this with Nature. I say if you can teach yourself to embrace and detach you can use the same technique for everything in life, to your benefit!

> **Foggy goggles are inevitable when wild swimming due to the changing temperature of your face and the water.** This makes sighting difficult so just move onto your back, lift your goggles up and swill with water to clear. Don't panic - it happens to us all!

Image: M. Flight

River Reading

Remember if you see dark, calm surface water this means there is depth to the water.

Large, fast rolling water, sometimes waves = large rocks, drop offs, possibly boulders below.

Small, rolling waves = shallow waters and smaller rocks below.

Large eddies and surface swirls = suggest something more powerful is happening below. These can be undercurrents (if you ever get caught in one of these – relax, tuck up into a ball to make yourself small and it will pop you out quicker. Never try to swim against it).

Don't be deceived - water on the Wye that looks calm has a stronger current than you think and is often underestimated. Decades of swimming this river has taught me to constantly look and listen above and below the water level, and stop and assess your route as this can be ever-changing with regard to weather conditions, debris, wildlife and other water users.

You can generally feel what's going on under the water with your feet and body. Remember you may be trying to read the river and avoid boulders and rapids while forgetting to look up. Often there are over hanging branches and debris close to the side!

Bridge pillars and ruins along the Wye collect a lot of debris and this can be far greater under water than you can see above so always assess and give a wide berth!

Fishing lines

Keep in mind that fishing lines are practically impossible to see, especially if the sun is glaring down or you are not paying attention.

Swim Techniques

Breaststroke and Front Crawl

Feel comfortable to choose your stroke, but please be aware that a wide, deep leg kick can be dangerous in the Wye due to underwater obstacles and lack of depth in many sections.

Your stroke should be as flat and streamlined as possible, with feet kept below the surface.

In both strokes the arm reach is long when gliding, which aids recovery and streamlines you, creating less resistance. Also, the pull back is your power and steering, so adapt to suit the different river sections.

Front crawl legs need to be balanced and relaxed. The key to saving energy, and vital for preventing that sinking feeling, is to alter strokes and technique to suit depth and distance.

Always protect your face as the odd unexpected underwater obstacle or over hanging branch does pop up and could knock you out! Nature will test you out to see if you are concentrating!

Tow floats can get tangled in debris, so be aware and as a last resort **unclip**! I have seen people make their own belts for their tow floats that are not quick release, which can result in entrapment.

Ottering and Swim Shallow

On certain sections of the Wye you will hear and see ripples closer to the surface which indicate shallow, small rapids that are quite common in this river, which is why looking, listening and feeling the power of the water is so crucial.

Lie on your back, feet up, hips up. Use your hand to steer and also hold your tow float onto your tummy to lift hips higher. This will get you over 10 inches of water, or even shallower.

Remember, going headfirst can lead to an unconscious swimmer. In large rapids go feet first all the time and as depth increases. Feel for the bottom with both hands for depth if visibility is poor.

Normally, the fastest part of the river is the centre, but often other river users can be in craft here. There is less resistance in the water closer to the edges; however, you need to be aware of fishermen, over hanging branches and debris.

Glide and Steer

Your hands are your paddles that will steer you through the water. The cup of your hand needs to be greater and tighter than when you swim in a pool. I've learnt the techniques of swimming in a foot of water and my arm pull and leg kick are very shallow to avoid hitting stones. This allows me to swim through the most technical of water sections safely.

The glide is so important for recovery and hands should cup the water after entry, in front of the shoulders. Rounded arm, long glide, the effort is underwater on the catch in open water.

Crocodile eyes (sighting / looking)

I regularly 'sight / look' as this is a crucial technique on the Wye with the amount of technical sections and obstacles. Using 'crocodile eyes' I look forward so my vision is reading below the surface and semi-

sighting then every few strokes, I lift my head higher to sight before I take a breath. As my hand enters the water, my other arm continues to recover out of the water.

> *"The solitude and freedom my monofin brings takes me to a different world below the surface and allows me to travel along the bed of the Wye.*
> *Exploring and seeking bring me great pleasure."*

Angela Jones

Free diving the Wye

A huge passion of mine lies below the surface of the Wye. We have some amazing deep salmon pools and stunning rock formations, where I have been watching and monitoring the life below the surface for decades. I've seen a huge decline in recent years which is very worrying (another reason to write this book).

If you do decide to have a look, please make sure you know the section, are competent and you can be seen with a tow float above the surface. So many people forget the beauty that lies beneath! This is also a fantastic way to increase lung capacity and I am a big believer in this practice.

Mike Lewis, age group European Championship/World Triathlon runner-up. This wonderful young man has volunteered with me over the years!

Swimming upstream against current

I so enjoy swimming against the current. It can be a great workout; and hugely helpful if you don't want to walk back or organise transport. It can also be great fun as you feel like you're on a conveyer belt and can hardly make any ground in some sections - these are marked on maps! Please take care, and note the gradings and conditions on the day.

Pool swimmer / wild swimmer?

Open water swimming can worry even experienced pool swimmers due to many factors. For example, the lack of lanes, depth, cold, what's in the water (fish and wildlife), currents, obstacles, poor visibility and not being able to touch the bottom or the sides.

Beware the Wye

The river looks so calm and serene, but it has strong currents and diverse technical sections that have taken many a life over the years and it is so underestimated.

Angela coaching in the pool

Hereford in flood

I've been swimming this river for over three decades and know all the sections inside out. I spend every day in it, except when it's in flood, both for work and play, normally clocking up 20 to 40 hours a week. I take and instruct hundreds of swimmers, of all ages and abilities!

I'm constantly asked for my advice and have rescued a number of swimmers. Sadly, fatalities are on the increase, which is why I wrote this book; **to make an enjoyable swim a safe one!**

PLEASE! People are throwing themselves in just anywhere without any knowledge of the immense danger they are putting themselves in. We have undercurrents (eddies), rapids, hidden boulders and debris, and the Wye is one of the fastest rising rivers at 30cm per hour. Look out for the many memorials along banks!

Open water swimming is one of the fastest growing sports in the UK and has increased dramatically since Covid-19. However, pool swimming is totally different to open water swimming! Weather conditions exhaust swimmers and hypothermia can easily set in. Please, please give the river due respect!

Severn Area Rescue Association (SARA) is one of the volunteer rescue charities which supports the fire services in conducting rescues from the River Wye. Each year there are emergency call outs, and sadly most years there are fatalities.

Stretches for Swimming in Nature's gym

To prevent injury, stretching is a very important and therapeutic exercise to do in Nature's Gym. Here I cover the main stretches that are beneficial for your arms, back, and legs. Hold each position for 30 seconds and repeat for both sides.

2 Elbow pull for your arm pit
For all four strokes we use our triceps, lats, and various shoulder muscles. Make sure you stretch them out really well. Here's how:

1. Place your right hand behind your head and point your elbow straight up.
2. Take your left hand and place it on your right elbow.
3. Pull your right elbow inward with your left hand.
4. Hold this position. Then switch arms and repeat.

1 Arms and shoulders
In all swim strokes you can't avoid using your arms and shoulders. That's why it's so important to stretch these out.

5 Tree lean for calves
Loosen up those calves. Here's how:

1. Place your hands on a tree at about shoulder-height. Keep your hands shoulder-width apart. Lean against the tree while facing toward it.
2. Scoot your right foot back as far as it can reach without straining it.
3. Place your right heel on the ground.
4. Keep your right leg straight.
5. Hold this position. Then switch legs and repeat.

3 Tree press for your front shoulder
The front of your shoulder is always a hard place to stretch. The tree press is a great way to access those hard-to-reach muscles. Follow these steps:

1. Place your right hand on a tree at shoulder height. Place your palm on the tree so your thumb is facing upward.
2. Slightly bend your right elbow.
3. Twist your body to your left — away from the tree.
4. Hold this position. Then switch arms and repeat.

4 Legs and buttocks
The kick propels us through the water, and we will likely rely on our legs and buttocks muscles extensively. Make sure you spend some time stretching out these muscles.

7 Butterfly stretch for your inner thigh and groin

Groin injuries can occur in swimming, especially in breaststroke. To help prevent inner thigh and groin injuries, make sure you stretch them out really well.

1. Sit up tall on the floor.
2. Bend your knees and relax your calves against the floor.
3. Press the soles of your feet together.
4. Hold your feet so that they remain touching. For a deeper stretch, press down on your knees.

6 Pretzel stretch for your buttocks

Believe it or not, you use your buttocks a lot in swimming. You use them while you kick, especially against strong currents. Follow these steps for a good pretzel stretch:

1. Sit down on the ground.
2. Bend your right leg and place the sole of your foot flat on the ground.
3. Lift your left leg up and place your left ankle on your right thigh.
4. Push your left knee away from you. If you're not feeling the stretch, scoot your right foot in closer to your buttocks.
5. Hold this position. Then switch legs and repeat.

8 Back

In freestyle you constantly rotate from side-to-side. This uses your laterals and lower back constantly. Spend some time stretching out your back to get your muscles feeling loose.

9 Model pose for your laterals

The model pose is a fantastic stretch to loosen up your tight laterals .

1. Sit on the floor.
2. Bend your left leg and place your left foot flat on the ground.
3. Straighten your right leg.
4. Cross your left foot over your right leg.
5. Take your right elbow and press it diagonally against the outside of your leg.
6. Push against your leg and twist your torso.
7. Hold this position. Then switch sides and repeat.

10 Child's pose for your lower back and hips

The child's pose will feel so good after a swim! Your lower back can feel increasingly sore after a long open water swim. This stretch accesses those lower back and hip muscles. Follow these steps for a good child's pose:

1. Kneel down, so that your whole shin is touching the floor.
2. Touch your legs together.

3. Rest your thighs on your calves.
4. Lean over your thighs so your belly touches your legs.
5. Lay your forehead on the ground.
6. Stretch your arms out in front of you with your palms facing downward.

11 After swim

It's so important to stretch after a swim and just take a few minutes to stretch out your muscles. Think about it as a warm-down and a loosen up. You'll feel great for when you next wild swim.

Image: S Pearce

Angela's Swim Sections

Over the last 30 years the Wye has shown me who is boss! And it is not me! The river can be calm and serene one minute, and then fast and furious the next.

Every section of the River Wye is hugely diverse and ever-changing. That is why I have chosen the swim sections presented in this book. I have graded each section and given as much information as I can, from many years of swimming them.

You can see my 86-mile journey Online on my YouTube channel, which the BBC covered as part of a documentary, filming me in my watery office. There was also an article about it in 'Outdoor Swimmer' (please see page 156).

Below Bigsweir Bridge, the Wye is tidal and too dangerous to swim. **Do not attempt to swim this section of the river**.

Image: S. Pearce

Swim section key indicates suitability

🚹 Family   ♿ Disabled access   🏊 Dip   🏊 Swim distance

Grading system

◼ Starting out/an enjoyable introduction to wild swimming.

◼ Moderate, experienced open water swimmer, 2 years' experience plus.

◼ Seasoned, hardened swimmer used to difficult long stretches, technical, fast-flowing sections and time in the water.

◼ Hazardous stretch, swim with extreme caution.

Wild swimming is not about being competent in swim speed, it is usually strength and time in the water and ability to read river signs that counts. In all sections of the Wye there are technical sections, so times and distances go out of the window.

The fastest section of the river is generally the centre; the edges are shallower but are prone to overhanging trees.

Wye Valley area map
Overview of map sections

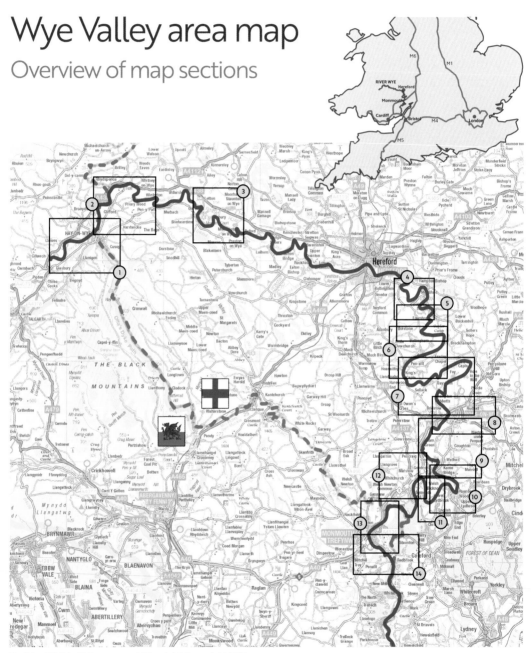

Contains OS data © Crown copyright and database right 2021

Swim sections map

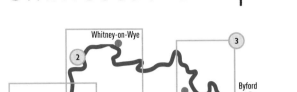

ANGELA'S ADVICE

- Study and assess your route and conditions
- Always know your entrance and your exit
- Relax, embrace and breath control
- Don't jump in. Ever. Cold water shock kills!

- Don't swim alone
- Make an emergency plan for quick exit and First Aid
- Know the signs for Hypothermia and how to treat
- Swim with a tow float, to be seen, carry kit and phone

- Get dressed and warm ASAP after your swim
- Look after each other
- Always respect the river and wildlife
- Have fun - life is for enjoying

Family time at The Warren

Family fun time at Glasbury Beach

Two wild women of the Wye. This crazy kindred spirit, Barbara Lewthwaite, taught me so much about reading this river

Serenity of a sunset over The Warren (Hay-on-Wye)

MAP 1

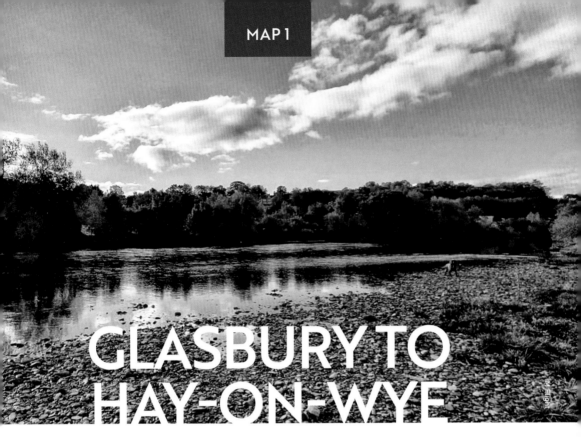

GLASBURY TO HAY-ON-WYE

Welcome to the wondrous Wye! We begin our first swim journey in the picturesque Welsh town of Glasbury, sometimes known as Glasbury-on-Wye, in the county of Powys. Glasbury is the point at which the River Wye connects Radnorshire and Brecknockshire, two historic counties.

At the start is an 800-metre swim section accessible from a large beach: this provides an ideal swim spot for families or a confidence builder if you are starting out on your river swimming journey.

Sitting north of the Brecon Beacons you'll enjoy a view of the Black Mountains along most of this section. You'll encounter some islands and fast-flowing rapids, so be careful at these points. The Warren is a well-known riverside meadow on the Welsh side of the Wales/England border where people picnic and enjoy the river: this is an ideal family area. The meadow has been declared a site of SSSI (Site of Special Scientific Interest). Do take some time to look out for wildlife as this part of the river is popular for Sand Martins, Egrets and Otters, which have been regularly seen.

This swim ends at Hay-on-Wye, a town famous for books and the annual Hay Festival.

Glasbury Bridge 800-metre swim section

Angela and Jack kayaking - Hay Bluff in the distance

Sand Martins nest in the banks along this section

MAP 1 · GLASBURY TO HAY-ON-WYE

GLASBURY

FOYLES HOTEL

Beach Area
A good training section to swim 800 metres upstream; also ideal for family dip.

Return walk
It is possible to walk back: however, undulating route so consider treating as a point to point swim. Leave a car at Hay-on-Wye and return to Glasbury by car.

Glasbury Bridge

GLASBURY BRIDGE

STAY ON THE WYE

△1 Busy section for kayaks and canoes.

△2 Be alert for fast-flowing rapids, islands and overhanging trees along this section.

△3 Weir in The Warren - exit water and walk around.

△4 Iron stakes on riverbed 100 metres below bridge at Hay-on-Wye.

DIGEDDI WILDLIFE CAMPSITE

HAY BLUFF

☆ Many entry points & car parking along this stretch so you can choose the length of your swim (seek permission).

Hay-on-Wye Bridge

The Warren
Ideal spot for a family day out. Dip and a picnic

THE WARREN P

HAY-ON-WYE

WEIR / BOULDERS

△3

RACQUETY FARM ⛺ P

△4 ☆

HAY BRIDGE P **WYEFORD**

KEY

☆ Swim Entrance / Exit
P Parking
👪 Family friendly
〰 Fast flowing water
⛺ Camping
🐟 Deep Salmon Pools
☕ Refreshment available
🛏 Places to stay
🍴 Places to eat
🍺 Places to drink
--- Indicates walk

SECTION: 1	DISTANCE	TIME (approx)	GRADE	ACTIVITY
GLASBURY TO HAY-ON-WYE	9.5k (5.9 miles)	1 hour 30 +	■	🏊
GLASBURY BEACH	or 800m upstream		▓ ░	🏊 👪 🤿

START POSTCODE: **HR3 5NP** FINISH POSTCODE: **HR3 5DH**
WYEFORD CAR PARK **HR3 5BJ** RACQUETY FARM CAR PARK **HR3 5RS**

MAPS ARE NOT TO SCALE, FOR ROUTE GUIDANCE ONLY

Wild flowers of the Wye

Hay-on-Wye Castle with the BBC filming my 5-week, 360 mile (kayak, run, swim) adventure along the River Wye

Angela's swim down to Whitney-on-Wye - half in Wales and half in England (the border is the middle of the Wye)

MAP 2

A Jones

HAY-ON-WYE TO BOAT INN

Hay-on-Wye Bridge

This Wild Wye swim is somewhat technical. The start,at Hay-on-Wye, is shallow and fast-flowing and is accessed via a ramp from Wyeford Bridge car park. The beautiful Water Crowfoot, an aquatic plant with stems of up to 20 feet long, can mat sections of this swim so remember to Glide, Relax and become part of the river.

Prior to the point where you cross the Wales/England border you are likely to be swimming in both countries as the borderline travels along the central part of the river before becoming England just after Clifford Castle (the Norman settlement built to protect the border). Take in the historic bridges as you pass under a derelict railway bridge and a 245-year-old toll bridge at Whitney-on-Wye (look out for the lucky black cat as you pass by). There are lots of long, dark, deep sections provided by the many salmon pools, as well as some fast-flowing sections which are guaranteed to provide some fun.

Shallow start section from Hay-on-Wye

Kingfisher - C. Lyons

Water Vole - D. Read

MAP 2 · HAY-ON-WYE TO BOAT INN

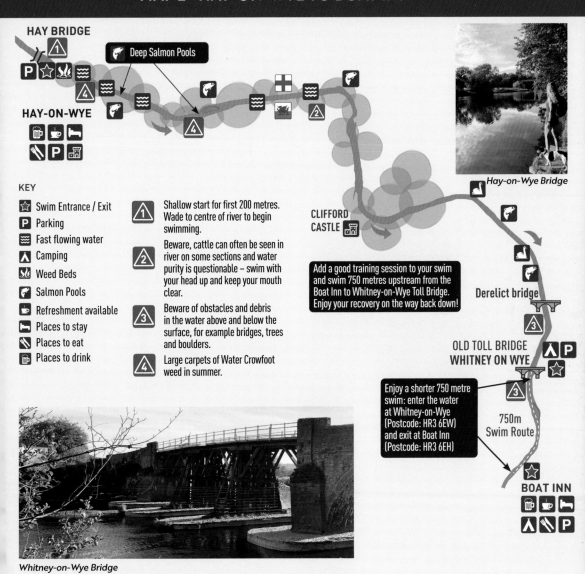

HAY BRIDGE

Deep Salmon Pools

HAY-ON-WYE

KEY

- ⭐ Swim Entrance / Exit
- 🅿 Parking
- ≋ Fast flowing water
- ⋀ Camping
- 🌿 Weed Beds
- 🐟 Salmon Pools
- ☕ Refreshment available
- 🛏 Places to stay
- 🔪 Places to eat
- 🍺 Places to drink

① Shallow start for first 200 metres. Wade to centre of river to begin swimming.

② Beware, cattle can often be seen in river on some sections and water purity is questionable – swim with your head up and keep your mouth clear.

③ Beware of obstacles and debris in the water above and below the surface, for example bridges, trees and boulders.

④ Large carpets of Water Crowfoot weed in summer.

CLIFFORD CASTLE

Add a good training session to your swim and swim 750 metres upstream from the Boat Inn to Whitney-on-Wye Toll Bridge. Enjoy your recovery on the way back down!

Hay-on-Wye Bridge

Derelict bridge

OLD TOLL BRIDGE WHITNEY ON WYE

Enjoy a shorter 750 metre swim: enter the water at Whitney-on-Wye (Postcode: HR3 6EW) and exit at Boat Inn (Postcode: HR3 6EH)

750m Swim Route

BOAT INN

Whitney-on-Wye Bridge

SECTION: 2	DISTANCE	TIME	GRADE	ACTIVITY
HAY-ON-WYE TO BOAT INN Wyeford Car Park	9.5k (5.9 miles)	1 hour 45 +	▢▢	🏊
BOAT INN TO WHITNEY ON WYE (upstream)	750 metres		▢▢	🏊
START POSTCODE: **HR3 5NP** FINISH POSTCODE: **HR3 6EH**				

MAPS ARE NOT TO SCALE, FOR ROUTE GUIDANCE ONLY

The Wye has many shallow sections with blankets of Water Crowfoot.

St Andrew's Church, Bredwardine

Sunset over the 200 feet high red sandstone cliffs of Brobury Scar

Jack enjoys the sun walking from the church to the bridge.

The beach at Bredwardine at the start of the 4-mile swim to Byecross Farm Campsite

MAP 3

BREDWARDINE TO BYECROSS FARM CAMPSITE

M Flight

This is a remote and breathtakingly stunning section which showcases the true beauty and diversity of the River Wye.

Travelling through isolated peaceful sections, deep salmon pools, fast-flowing rapids and boulders, you will experience some of the most picturesque and magical landscapes along the River Wye. In particular, swimming alongside ancient woodlands and the stunning high, red sandstone cliffs of Brobury Scar before Moccas Court.

ANGELA'S THOUGHTS

Bredwardine to Byecross This committed section offers miles of beautiful, isolated river. Depending on conditions, the initial section is shallow so water shoes are a must. The wildlife is captivating, and you may see Dippers, Kingfishers and leaping Salmon, to name but a few. You'll swim beneath 200-feet red sandstone cliffs, past high banks and gravel beaches and encounter several large boulders in the riverbed to remind you the Wye is boss! And look out for a glimpse of the remains of Mocca toll bridge. You will recognise your exit on the right by the vibrant red sandstone flats at Byecross Farm Campsite. I highly recommend this well-equipped campsite that welcomes visitors from the river and is open from February to October. Treat this as a point-to-point swim, leaving a vehicle at the campsite but please seek permission from owners Tony and Sharon Fenn to park here (fee applicable).

Angela swims past red sandstone slabs at Byecross Farm Campsite exit

Relaxing in the meadows (St Andrew's Church, Bredwardine)

Ancient woodland at Brobury Scar

MAP 3 · BREDWARDINE TO BYECROSS FARM CAMPSITE

Ideal family area for a picnic and a paddle in low river level conditions

ST ANDREW'S CHURCH

BREDWARDINE

BROBURY HOUSE & GARDENS

Brobury Scar Red Sandstone Cliffs

200 feet high red sandstone cliffs at Brobury Scar

Ideal family area for a picnic and a paddle in low river level conditions at Byecross Farm.

MONNINGTON ON WYE

MOCCAS PARK NATIONAL NATURE RESERVE

Red Sandstone Slabs

BYECROSS FARM CAMPSITE
PRESTON ON WYE

Bredwardine Bridge

Red sandstone flats at Byecross Farm Campsite

KEY

- ⭐ Swim Entrance / Exit
- 🅿 Parking
- 👪 Family friendly
- 〰 Fast flowing water
- 🐟 Salmon Pools
- ⛺ Camping
- ☕ Refreshment available
- ✝ Church
- --- Indicates walk

 Take care walking down to gravel beach, the bank is worn and steep.

 Start can be shallow depending on time of year so please take care.

 Beware of rapids created by shallow rocky areas.

OPEN WATER SWIMMER'S THOUGHTS

The swim itself provides plenty of quiet reflection and moments of amazement. The wildlife, both flora and fauna, is exemplary of Herefordshire. Kingfishers, Heron, numerous varieties of Duck, Swans, leaping Salmon and Tiddlers. The conditions when I swam were quiet, so it was a real swim with only occasional times over rapids using the 'ottering' technique. To create 'whole body sticks' was essential but the contrast when swimming over a deep pool was so wonderful these presented no real issues. The wildlife was one thing; however, the scenery was stunning, especially swimming below the Scar before Moccas Court, which was a unique experience.

SECTION: 3	DISTANCE	TIME	GRADE	ACTIVITY
BREDWARDINE TO BYECROSS FARM CAMPSITE	6.6k (4.1 miles)	1.30 hours +	■	🏊 👪

START POSTCODE: **HR3 6BS** (opposite Brobury House)   FINISH POSTCODE: **HR2 9LJ** (Byecross Campsite)
Family picnic and paddle postcode: **HR3 6BT** (St Andrew's Church)

S Pearce

Angela on 800-metre swim down to the Bunch of Carrots at Hampton Bishop.

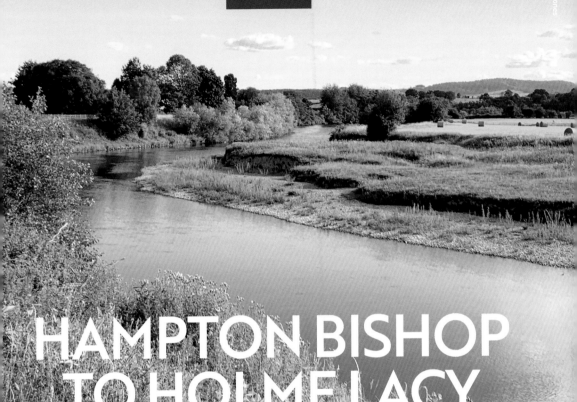

MAP 4

HAMPTON BISHOP TO HOLME LACY

Hampton Bishop to Holme Lacy is another committed swim section for stronger open water swimmers. There are many deep salmon pools along this section and some technical, fast-flowing waters to tackle that need the technique of ottering (feet first, hips high) allowing you safety and the ability to swim in the shallowest of rapids. Fishing lines are plentiful in the latter section so stay alert; regular sighting is essential.

You will notice a drop in temperature as the River Lugg joins the Wye from the left-hand side, about 500 metres before reaching Holme Lacy Bridge. This modern road bridge crosses the water before the pontoon, which indicates the exit point to Lucksall Campsite on the left-hand side. 800 metres further downstream there is another pontoon, where you could exit onto the campsite if you want to swim a little further. This is a popular area of the river for Sand Martins nesting in the banks, Herons, Egrets, Kingfishers, and I've even caught sight of the odd Terrapin. The Swans are plentiful and some of them are quite inquisitive, especially when you arrive at Lucksall Campsite.

Swim down to Holme Lacy

Pontoon exit at Lucksall Campsite (Holme Lacy)

Jack in ancient woodland

MAP 4 · HAMPTON BISHOP TO HOLME LACY

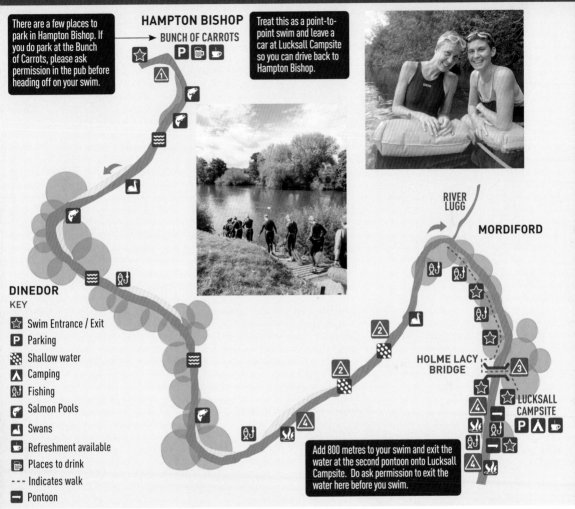

There are a few places to park in Hampton Bishop. If you do park at the Bunch of Carrots, please ask permission in the pub before heading off on your swim.

HAMPTON BISHOP
BUNCH OF CARROTS

Treat this as a point-to-point swim and leave a car at Lucksall Campsite so you can drive back to Hampton Bishop.

RIVER LUGG

MORDIFORD

DINEDOR

KEY

⭐ Swim Entrance / Exit

🅿 Parking

▨ Shallow water

⛺ Camping

🎣 Fishing

🐟 Salmon Pools

🦢 Swans

☕ Refreshment available

🍺 Places to drink

--- Indicates walk

▬ Pontoon

HOLME LACY BRIDGE

LUCKSALL CAMPSITE

Add 800 metres to your swim and exit the water at the second pontoon onto Lucksall Campsite. Do ask permission to exit the water here before you swim.

 Entering deep water near the Bunch of Carrots, you can swim 800 metres upstream for an out and back workout or choose the 4-mile swim down to Holme Lacy.

 Water shoes are highly recommended for this section; due to shallow areas you may need to navigate on foot.

 Be aware of debris at foot of Holme Lacy Bridge and swim in the middle to avoid any potential hazards.

 Possible entanglement from Water Crowfoot Weed.

SECTION: 4	DISTANCE	TIME	GRADE	ACTIVITY
HAMPTON BISHOP TO HOLME LACY	7k (4.3 miles)	1.30 hours +		
HOLME LACY TO MORDIFORD	800 metres upstream			
START POSTCODE: **HR1 4JR** (Bunch of Carrots) FINISH POSTCODE: **HR1 4LP** (Lucksall Campsite)				

MAPS ARE NOT TO SCALE, FOR ROUTE GUIDANCE ONLY

In the golden mile of fishing

Angela's 4k walk back from Fownhope to Holme Lacy

Swim down from Holme Lacy to Fownhope

MAP 5

S Pearce

HOLME LACY TO FOWNHOPE

Entrance at Holme Lacy Bridge

**Holme Lacy to Fownhope is a glorious 2.8-mile route.
Enter at the Holme Lacy Bridge or off one of the two deep water pontoons at Lucksall Campsite.**

The river meanders and there are several deep sections providing stretches of quiet swims, where you can absorb yourself in the beauty of the surroundings and wildlife. Fast, shallow sections provide the ideal opportunity for you to practice your technical river swimming skills, such as ottering feet first, hips high, and steering with your sculling hands. Sighting is paramount on this section as there are often cattle drinking and many fishermen on route, with the added delight of swans in abundance. You could leave a vehicle at Fownhope Pavilion and Recreation Field car park and drive back to Lucksall Campsite. I enjoy the picturesque 4k walk back but beware, you need to cross a busy country road. Lucksall Campsite is set in a gorgeous location of 21 acres, on the bank of the river, and there is an on-site restaurant and shop, which makes it a perfect place to stay, or as an entrance and exit for swims. Please seek permission from the owners to park and enter the water here (fee applicable).

Angela's sunset swim down to Fownhope

Image: M. Cray

Heron enjoying a deep salmon pool in the golden mile

MAP 5 · HOLME LACY TO FOWNHOPE

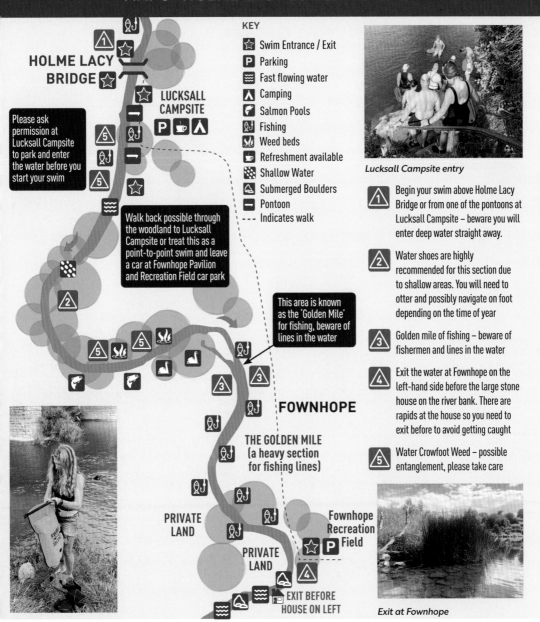

KEY

⭐	Swim Entrance / Exit
P	Parking
≋	Fast flowing water
⛰	Camping
🐟	Salmon Pools
🎣	Fishing
🌿	Weed beds
☕	Refreshment available
▓	Shallow Water
◺	Submerged Boulders
▬	Pontoon
---	Indicates walk

HOLME LACY BRIDGE

LUCKSALL CAMPSITE

Please ask permission at Lucksall Campsite to park and enter the water before you start your swim

Walk back possible through the woodland to Lucksall Campsite or treat this as a point-to-point swim and leave a car at Fownhope Pavilion and Recreation Field car park

This area is known as the 'Golden Mile' for fishing, beware of lines in the water

FOWNHOPE

THE GOLDEN MILE (a heavy section for fishing lines)

PRIVATE LAND

PRIVATE LAND

Fownhope Recreation Field

EXIT BEFORE HOUSE ON LEFT

Lucksall Campsite entry

1. Begin your swim above Holme Lacy Bridge or from one of the pontoons at Lucksall Campsite – beware you will enter deep water straight away.

2. Water shoes are highly recommended for this section due to shallow areas. You will need to otter and possibly navigate on foot depending on the time of year

3. Golden mile of fishing – beware of fishermen and lines in the water

4. Exit the water at Fownhope on the left-hand side before the large stone house on the river bank. There are rapids at the house so you need to exit before to avoid getting caught

5. Water Crowfoot Weed – possible entanglement, please take care

Exit at Fownhope

Kitting Up, Holme Lacy Bridge

SECTION: 5		DISTANCE	TIME	GRADE	ACTIVITY
HOLME LACY TO FOWNHOPE		4.5k (2.8 miles)	45 mins +	▢ ▢	🏊 🏊
START POSTCODE: **HR1 4LP** (Lucksall Campsite)		FINISH POSTCODE: **HR1 4PE** (Fownhope Recreation Field)			

MAPS ARE NOT TO SCALE, FOR ROUTE GUIDANCE ONLY

First fast 300-metre technical section of swim, Fownhope

Fownhope

Image: M. Flight

Carey Bridge, a demolished railway bridge, is one of three bridges crossing the Wye between Ross and Hereford (closed in 1964)

MAP 6

FOWNHOPE TO HOARWITHY

Entrance point from Fownhope to Hoarwithy

This swim is very technical and needs a great deal of Wye experience and sighting!

Over the first 400 metres are fast rapids, large boulders and overhanging trees, so ottering is a must. Again, 1.8k to 2.5k is another fast, technical section, with several large meanders and long, deep sections with many fishermen on the left bank. 6.5k into this swim you come to Carey Islands: keep right normally at the first island, then 500 metres downstream there's the old, demolished railway bridge which often accumulates plenty of debris at the base. At 9k you come to Bibletts nature reserve, where there is usually a shallow beach that is ideal for families to picnic and dip. Continue under Hoarwithy Bridge to Tresseck Campsite, where you exit on right. Dappled Fallow Deer can often be seen along this section, with a large variety of birds that inhabit the woodlands. Kingfishers are plentiful in this area.

OTHER SWIM OPTIONS

You have options on this route:

- Walk up to Carey Bridge from Hoarwithy and swim back 3.5k, grade 2
- Bibletts to Hoarwithy 750 metre, grade 1 / 2 • Carey Bridge to Bibletts 2.5k, grade 2
- Family swim and picnics ideal at Bibletts Nature Reserve or enjoy Tresseck Campsite, the perfect riverside location. This family-owned campsite is run by Jeff and Sarah Goulding and their children, who are passionate about preserving the environment of our wonderful Wye.

Family fun on the beach below Carey

Family beach Bibletts (Hoarwithy) at low water

Swan gliding majestically along the Wye, rough waters at Fownhope entrance.

MAP 6 · FOWNHOPE TO HOARWITHY

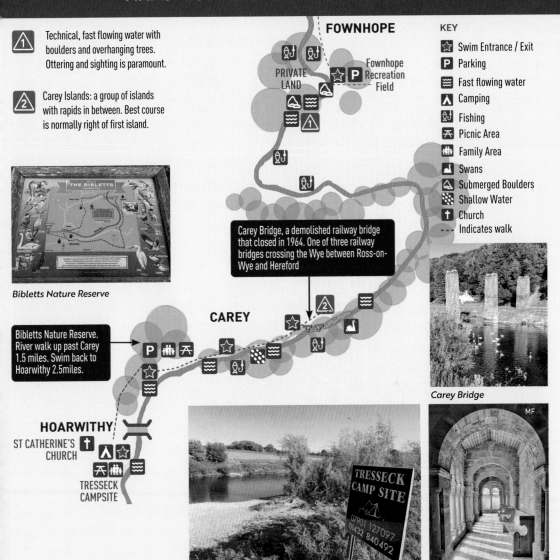

1 Technical, fast flowing water with boulders and overhanging trees. Ottering and sighting is paramount.

2 Carey Islands: a group of islands with rapids in between. Best course is normally right of first island.

FOWNHOPE

KEY

⭐ Swim Entrance / Exit
🅿 Parking
▦ Fast flowing water
⛺ Camping
🎣 Fishing
🧺 Picnic Area
👪 Family Area
🦢 Swans
🌊 Submerged Boulders
▨ Shallow Water
✝ Church
--- Indicates walk

PRIVATE LAND

Fownhope Recreation Field

Bibletts Nature Reserve

Carey Bridge, a demolished railway bridge that closed in 1964. One of three railway bridges crossing the Wye between Ross-on-Wye and Hereford

CAREY

Bibletts Nature Reserve. River walk up past Carey 1.5 miles. Swim back to Hoarwithy 2.5miles.

Carey Bridge

HOARWITHY
ST CATHERINE'S CHURCH

TRESSECK CAMPSITE

Campsite and beach at Hoarwithy

St Catherine's Church, Hoarwithy (1840)

SECTION: 6	DISTANCE	TIME	GRADE	ACTIVITY
FOWNHOPE TO HOARWITHY	10.6k (6.6 miles)	2 hours +	■	🏊
CAREY TO HOARWITHY	4K (2.5 miles)	45 min	▨	🏊 👪 🏊
BIBLETTS TO HOARWITHY	750m	15 min	▨	🏊 👪 🏊

START POSTCODE: **HR1 4PE** (Fownhope recreation field) FINISH POSTCODE: **HR2 6QH** (Tresseck Campsite)

MAPS ARE NOT TO SCALE, FOR ROUTE GUIDANCE ONLY

Hoarwithy beach entrance at Tresseck Campsite

Exits both sides of river at Backney derelict railway bridge

Angela swimming under Sellack Bridge

MAP 7

M Flight

HOARWITHY TO BACKNEY COMMON

A vicar in earlier times used stilts to cross the Wye to avoid a lengthy detour. The Victorian Bridge at Sellack replaced a ferry that was once used here.

As you enter the water at Tresseck Campsite, the current can sometimes be strong. Swim down on the right-hand side for the first few hundred metres; you'll pass a few shingle beaches then a wonderful 2-mile swim with not too many technical sections. Some of this 2-mile section runs parallel to the walk back route so you could exit the swim early if you require.

Sellack to Foy Bridge swimming through Hole-in-the-Wall is 2 miles. This is private land with many deep salmon pools - beware of fishing lines! As you swim from Sellack, about 1 mile downstream you'll come to the Strangford demolished railway bridge; beware of debris around the pillars. You will then meet a few fast-flowing rapid sections and some islands with fast flowing water where constant assessing and ottering is essential – mainly stay right.

The beautiful suspension bridge at Foy allows no exits as it is surrounded by private land. Under the bridge at Foy are small, fast-flowing rapids, then you are quickly into an island where you stay right and meander down the river for another mile before coming to the derelict railway bridge at Brampton Abbotts. The wildlife in this section is particularly stunning! An array of birds, many nesting, include Sand Martins (April – September).

200 metres before the derelict Backney railway bridge, cattle are often drinking at the water's edge. Beware, and heads-up swimming is required! Exits either side; car parking at Backney Common is on the right-hand side. On the left-hand side there is a beautiful 2-mile walk back to Ross-on- Wye that runs parallel to the river.

Foy Bridge (1876) was washed away by floods and replaced in 1921

Church at Sellack dedicated to St. Tysilio (or St. Tesiliog) Tysilio and Sulac are both pet forms of the Welsh personal name Suliau

Angela talking to salmon specialist about the impact of wild swimming and fishing at Foy Bridge

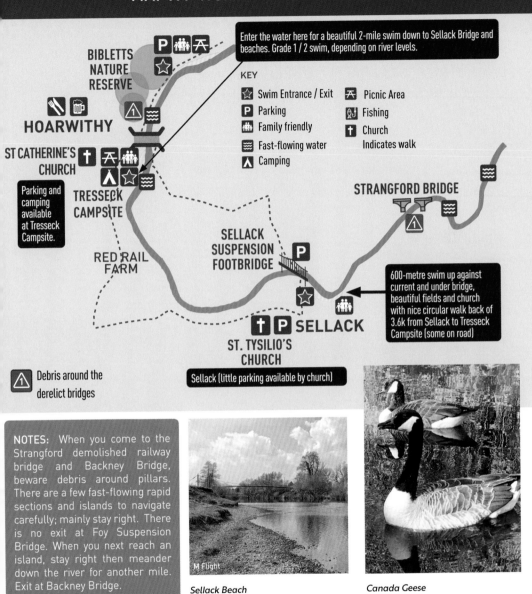

BIBLETTS NATURE RESERVE

Enter the water here for a beautiful 2-mile swim down to Sellack Bridge and beaches. Grade 1 / 2 swim, depending on river levels.

HOARWITHY

KEY

☆	Swim Entrance / Exit	🏕	Picnic Area
P	Parking	🎣	Fishing
👪	Family friendly	✝	Church
≋	Fast-flowing water		Indicates walk
⋀	Camping		

ST CATHERINE'S CHURCH

Parking and camping available at Tresseck Campsite.

TRESSECK CAMPSITE

STRANGFORD BRIDGE

RED RAIL FARM

SELLACK SUSPENSION FOOTBRIDGE

600-metre swim up against current and under bridge, beautiful fields and church with nice circular walk back of 3.6k from Sellack to Tresseck Campsite (some on road)

SELLACK

ST. TYSILIO'S CHURCH

Sellack (little parking available by church)

⚠ Debris around the derelict bridges

NOTES: When you come to the Strangford demolished railway bridge and Backney Bridge, beware debris around pillars. There are a few fast-flowing rapid sections and islands to navigate carefully; mainly stay right. There is no exit at Foy Suspension Bridge. When you next reach an island, stay right then meander down the river for another mile. Exit at Backney Bridge.

Sellack Beach

M Flight

Canada Geese

MAP 7B Shows the Sellack to Backney Bridge stretch. This is a long committed technical swim with **NO early exits**.

SECTION: 7	DISTANCE	TIME (approx)	GRADE	ACTIVITY
HOARWITHY TO SELLACK	3.5k (2 miles)	45 mins +		🏊 👪 🌊
SELLACK BEACH (optional)	600m swim upstream			🏊 👪 🌊
START POSTCODE: **HR2 6QH** (Tresseck Campsite) FINISH POSTCODE: **HR9 6LT** (St Tysilio's Church, Sellack)				

"This magnificent river is to be enjoyed and respected. We are merely guests, invited to enjoy its beauty only if we truly share passion for the environment and respect for the biodiversity of the wonderful Wye."

Image: M Flight

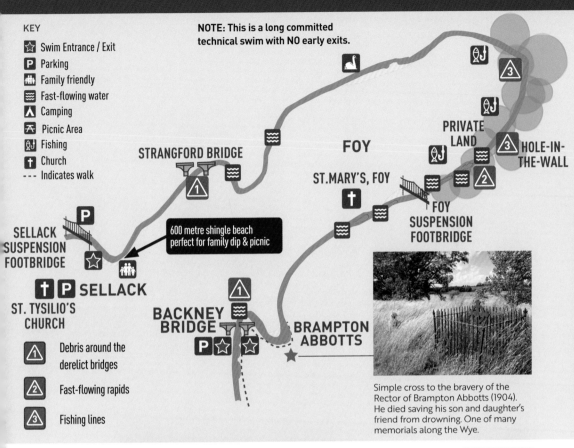

KEY

- ⭐ Swim Entrance / Exit
- 🅿 Parking
- 👪 Family friendly
- 〰 Fast-flowing water
- ⋀ Camping
- ⛱ Picnic Area
- 🎣 Fishing
- ✝ Church
- --- Indicates walk

NOTE: This is a long committed technical swim with NO early exits.

STRANGFORD BRIDGE

FOY

ST. MARY'S, FOY

FOY SUSPENSION FOOTBRIDGE

PRIVATE LAND

HOLE-IN-THE-WALL

SELLACK SUSPENSION FOOTBRIDGE

600 metre shingle beach perfect for family dip & picnic

SELLACK

ST. TYSILIO'S CHURCH

BACKNEY BRIDGE

BRAMPTON ABBOTTS

⚠1 Debris around the derelict bridges

⚠2 Fast-flowing rapids

⚠3 Fishing lines

Simple cross to the bravery of the Rector of Brampton Abbotts (1904). He died saving his son and daughter's friend from drowning. One of many memorials along the Wye.

Angela swimming at Foy Bridge

SECTION: 7	DISTANCE	TIME (approx)	GRADE	ACTIVITY
SELLACK TO BACKNEY COMMON	9k (5.75miles)	1 hour 45 mins +	■	🏊

START POSTCODE: **HR9 6LT** (St Tysilio's Church, Sellack)   FINISH POSTCODE: **HR9 6RD** Backney Picnic Site

Hole-in-the-Wall - Sellack to Foy. This section is private land. Many fishermen enjoy fishing along this stretch.

Image: M. Flight

Angela swimming to Ross-on-Wye

S Pearce

104

MAP 8

BACKNEY TO ROSS-ON-WYE

Cygnets on the river bank below Ross Rowing Club

This spectacular swim takes you along the river as it meanders through tree-lined banks into the picturesque market town of Ross-on-Wye, with its landmark of St Mary's Church steeple standing high on the hill.

There's plenty of parking in Ross-on-Wye and you can get fairly close to the river. I recommend the car park at The Hope & Anchor Inn; alternatively, park on the roadside at Wye Street (public toilets here). Walk the Wye Valley Walk parallel to the river through the park, past Ross Rowing Club and up to Backney Common (3k). While walking, notice the various entry and exit points and beaches along the river, just in case you want to have a shorter swim. The path bends right as you reach the derelict pillar remains of Backney Railway Bridge. The swim entrance is off a beach before the pillars. This fast-flowing section soon smooths out. 1k downstream it speeds up and I find the right-hand side has less big

rocks to otter. Swim through wide, tree-lined sections before swimming underneath the A40 bridge and you will see the famous spire of St Mary's Church that has sat high on the skyline for 700 years. The river widens and you'll pass a large beach which runs down to Ross Rowing Club (keep an eye out for rowers on the water). The exit is on the left, 100 metres below The Hope & Anchor Inn. Beware of the uneven floor and concrete platform that was damaged during the 2020 flooding. A second exit is 300 metres further downstream on the left, but beware, currents can be very strong!

Fields of Gold on Wye Valley Walk

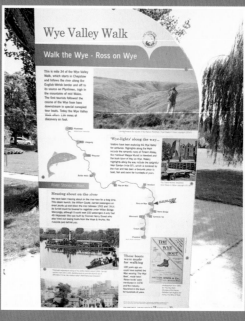
Sign on riverbank at Ross, at second stated exit point

Swimming downstream under A40 bridge into Ross-on-Wye

Exit pontoon at Hope & Anchor

MAP 8 · BACKNEY TO ROSS-ON-WYE

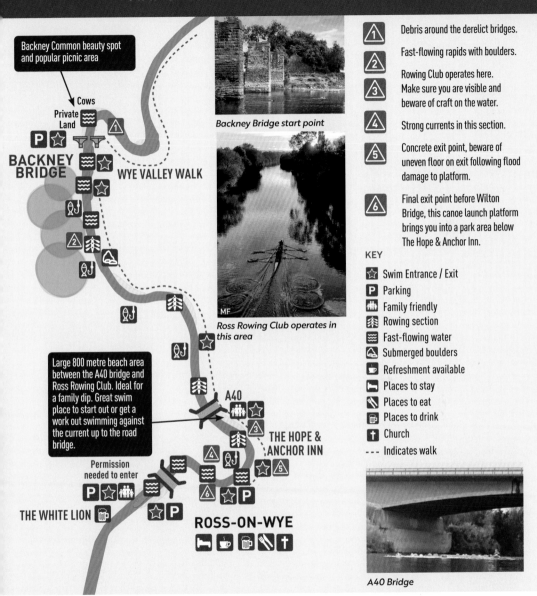

Backney Bridge start point

Ross Rowing Club operates in this area

Backney Common beauty spot and popular picnic area

Cows
Private Land

BACKNEY BRIDGE

WYE VALLEY WALK

Large 800 metre beach area between the A40 bridge and Ross Rowing Club. Ideal for a family dip. Great swim place to start out or get a work out swimming against the current up to the road bridge.

A40

THE HOPE & ANCHOR INN

Permission needed to enter

THE WHITE LION

ROSS-ON-WYE

1 Debris around the derelict bridges.

2 Fast-flowing rapids with boulders.

3 Rowing Club operates here. Make sure you are visible and beware of craft on the water.

4 Strong currents in this section.

5 Concrete exit point, beware of uneven floor on exit following flood damage to platform.

6 Final exit point before Wilton Bridge, this canoe launch platform brings you into a park area below The Hope & Anchor Inn.

KEY

☆ Swim Entrance / Exit
P Parking
Family friendly
Rowing section
Fast-flowing water
Submerged boulders
Refreshment available
Places to stay
Places to eat
Places to drink
† Church
--- Indicates walk

A40 Bridge

SECTION: 8	DISTANCE	TIME	GRADE	ACTIVITY
BACKNEY TO ROSS-ON-WYE	3k – 3.5k depending on exit	40 mins +		
BEACH BY ROWING CLUB TO A40 BRIDGE	600m swim upstream			

START POSTCODE: **HR9 6QX** (Backney Common)   FINISH POSTCODE: **HR9 7BX** (The Hope & Anchor Inn, Ross)

MAPS ARE NOT TO SCALE, FOR ROUTE GUIDANCE ONLY

Angela starting swim down to Ross-on-Wye at Backney

Image: S Pearce

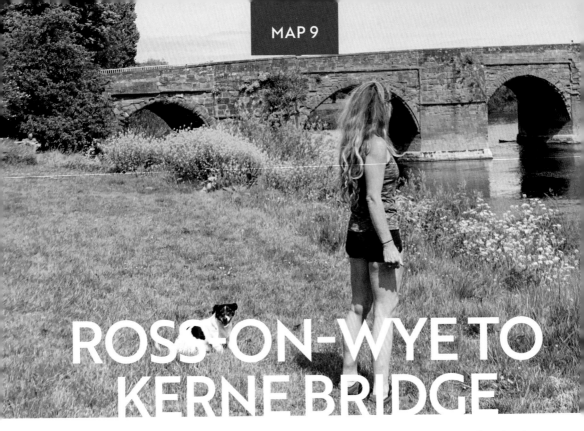

MAP 9

ROSS-ON-WYE TO KERNE BRIDGE

This spectacular swim is a great route for landmarks. Beginning in the historic market town of Ross-on-Wye, swimming under the historic 13th century Wilton Bridge, that crosses the river on the entrance to the town and high on the hill the view of the Norman medieval castle at Goodrich, and finally swimming under the iconic 5 pillars of Kerne Bridge, built in 1825.

There is a scenic, circular riverside walk from Wilton Road car park (HR9 5JA). Park all day for £1 and walk to access several shingle beaches, which are ideal for a family picnic and dip. These beaches provide ideal access to the river to begin your swim down to Kerne Bridge. They also allow you to avoid the shallow, fast-flowing section under Wilton Bridge if you were starting your swim from The Hope & Anchor Inn at Ross-on-Wye. I recommend treating this as a point-to-point swim, leaving a vehicle at Kerne Bridge Canoe Launch, where there is ample parking (fee applicable), so you can drive back to the start. There are several fast, shallow sections that need ottering (feet first, hips high, sculling with hands). Constant assessing for strong undercurrents and eddies is crucial in this section. If you get caught in an eddy don't try and swim out of it as exhaustion can set in; tuck up

into a ball and it will soon pop you out! When swimming over blankets of Water Crowfoot Weed don't kick, just glide to avoid entrapment. There is a beach 1k before Kerne Bridge, on the right, if you don't want to tackle the fast-flowing water immediately after Kerne Bridge. You could walk back the 7k here to Ross: just follow the path parallel to the river all the way back to Ross-on-Wye. Before you swim under Kerne Bridge, stop and assess the water since it can catch you out here as it speeds up, with underlying obstacles and overhanging trees. There is an exit on the right-hand side, just after Kerne Bridge, where there is a lovely family picnic and dip section, but the water can be sometimes seriously fast-flowing. Alternatively, you can add an extra 800 metres to your swim and exit left at Kerne Bridge Canoe Launch (be careful of the large rocks in the water by the concrete exit platform).

ANGELA'S VIEW

Beautiful, meandering 9k river swim with several shallow, fast-flowing sections for ottering, deep salmon pools and wide, long stretches to lose yourself in the magnificent and serene part of the Wye. Be warned; this route has ways of reminding you who's boss, so take extra care of undercurrents!

Support crew recciing my Wye 86-mile swim route

Angela swims down at Kerne Bridge

Family fun on one of many shallow beaches below Wilton Bridge

MAP 9 · ROSS-ON-WYE TO KERNE BRIDGE

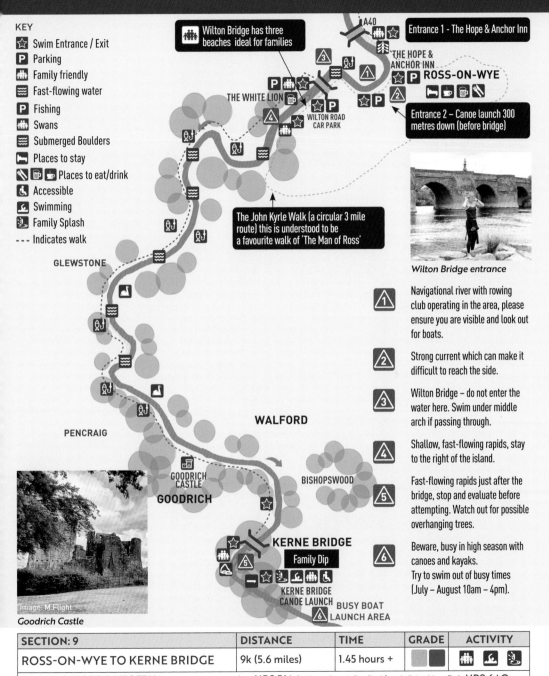

KEY

- ⭐ Swim Entrance / Exit
- 🅿 Parking
- 👪 Family friendly
- 〰 Fast-flowing water
- 🅿 Fishing
- 🦢 Swans
- 〰 Submerged Boulders
- 🛏 Places to stay
- 🍽 Places to eat/drink
- ♿ Accessible
- 🏊 Swimming
- 🤽 Family Splash
- - - - Indicates walk

Wilton Bridge has three beaches ideal for families

THE WHITE LION

WILTON ROAD CAR PARK

The John Kyrle Walk (a circular 3 mile route) this is understood to be a favourite walk of 'The Man of Ross'

Entrance 1 - The Hope & Anchor Inn

THE HOPE & ANCHOR INN

ROSS-ON-WYE

Entrance 2 – Canoe launch 300 metres down (before bridge)

Wilton Bridge entrance

GLEWSTONE

PENCRAIG

WALFORD

GOODRICH CASTLE

GOODRICH

BISHOPSWOOD

Image: M.Flight

Goodrich Castle

KERNE BRIDGE

Family Dip

KERNE BRIDGE CANOE LAUNCH

BUSY BOAT LAUNCH AREA

1️⃣ Navigational river with rowing club operating in the area, please ensure you are visible and look out for boats.

2️⃣ Strong current which can make it difficult to reach the side.

3️⃣ Wilton Bridge – do not enter the water here. Swim under middle arch if passing through.

4️⃣ Shallow, fast-flowing rapids, stay to the right of the island.

5️⃣ Fast-flowing rapids just after the bridge, stop and evaluate before attempting. Watch out for possible overhanging trees.

6️⃣ Beware, busy in high season with canoes and kayaks.
Try to swim out of busy times (July – August 10am – 4pm).

SECTION: 9	DISTANCE	TIME	GRADE	ACTIVITY
ROSS-ON-WYE TO KERNE BRIDGE	9k (5.6 miles)	1.45 hours +		👪 🏊 🤽

START POSTCODE: **HR9 7BX** (Hope & Anchor Inn) or **HR9 5JA** (Wilton Road Car Park) or White Lion Pub **HR9 6AQ**
FINISH POSTCODE: **HR9 5QX** (Kerne Bridge Canoe Launch)

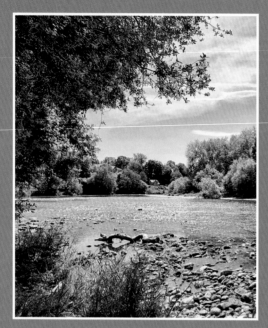

River Wye between Ross-on-Wye and Kerne Bridge

White Lion, Wilton Bridge, Ross-on-Wye

Kingfisher enjoys a minnow from the Wye

Angela kitting up for a 9k swim to Kerne Bridge

Kerne Bridge   Image: M Flight

'Swans will break your arms!' How many times have I heard this?

The heaviest flying bird is not always what it's made out to be! Swans are not aggressive creatures, they simply defend their young and territory! We are merely guests in their habitat, so please respect and pass quietly by these beautiful birds. If they display their wings, it's a warning! If their neck goes back, they feel threatened. In all my years on the Wye neither swans nor Canada Geese have attacked me! Respect. Canada Geese land early spring and I've got to know the groups along the river. It's always a joyous, welcome sight. One particular group, for the last eight years near Symonds Yat, has had a lone white goose join them. After asking Iolo Williams, nature expert, he informs me it would have absconded from a farm. I wish humans would follow Nature's unprejudiced view!

Image: G.K. Wood

Swim down to Lydbrook at dusk

Swim Wild Wye guided swim from Kerne Bridge to Lydbrook

Angela swimming to Lydbrook

Entrance at Kerne Bridge Canoe Launch

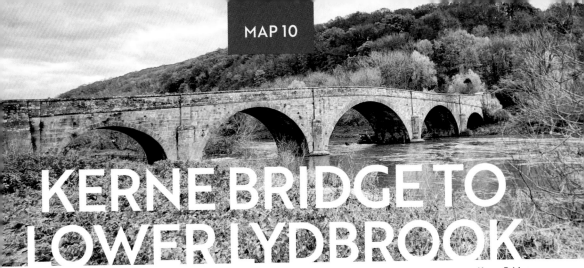

MAP 10

KERNE BRIDGE TO LOWER LYDBROOK

Kerne Bridge

Another stunning swim section is from Kerne Bridge Canoe Launch down to Lower Lydbrook. This is an isolated committed section, with few early exits so not advisable for beginners.

The Canoe Launch is an ideal starting point as there is a disabled access ramp to the water's edge which allows you to gently enter the water. An alternative way to add 1k to your swim is to park at the Canoe Launch and walk upstream along the Wye Valley Walk and enter the water at the iconic Kerne Bridge. However, be aware of strong flowing rapids for the first few hundred metres, and low branches. There are shallow, fast rapids to tackle 2k into this swim, and faster, more furious rapids as you near Lower Lydbrook. Make sure you otter in these sections - feet first and hips high! Wildlife in this section is plentiful due to high banks and quiet stretches. Look out for Kingfisher, Canada Geese, leaping Salmon, Egrets, Herons and Mandarin Ducks to name just a few. This is a popular stretch of water for fishermen and many novice canoeists in the summer months, so ensure you are visible by wearing a bright hat and tow float. Be alert to collisions at the rapids in heavy water traffic! Before reaching Lower Lydbrook you'll need to go to the left of the large island to avoid the overhanging trees and rapids. Water shoes are advisable as wading is needed to exit the water at the concrete pontoon, where there are steps up to an ideal family picnic spot and car park overlooking the river.

ANGELA'S THOUGHTS

Park at Kerne Bridge Canoe Launch (Charlie, the owner, welcomes swimmers). Enter at the Canoe Launch or walk 800m along the Wye Valley Walk which runs parallel to the river and takes you up to Kerne Bridge. Enter here or add an extra 1k swim by walking a little further up the riverbank, where you'll spot a beach. From here, you can enjoy a longer swim under Kerne Bridge before taking on this stunning swim section to Lydbrook. Beware, this is not a swim for beginners as it's technical and fast-rolling in places! This swim has caught many a novice out and rescue teams have been called to assist.

Lower Lydbrook island and shallow rapids (exit on left)

Entrance at Kerne Bridge Canoe Launch

Egrets are often seen in this stretch (pictured: Little Egret, identified by its yellow feet)

MAP 10 · KERNE BRIDGE TO LOWER LYDBROOK

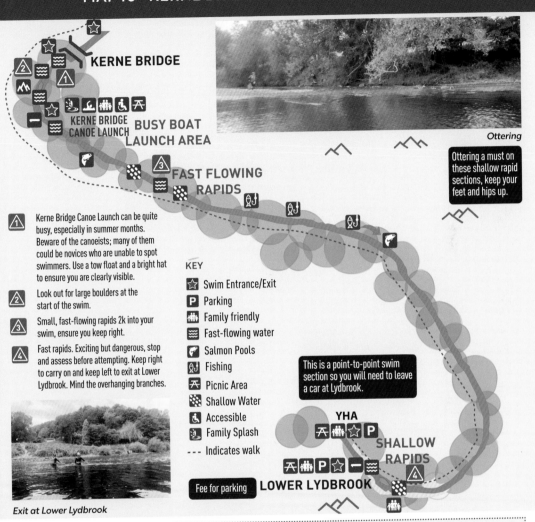

KERNE BRIDGE

KERNE BRIDGE CANOE LAUNCH

BUSY BOAT LAUNCH AREA

FAST FLOWING RAPIDS

Ottering

Ottering a must on these shallow rapid sections, keep your feet and hips up.

⚠1 Kerne Bridge Canoe Launch can be quite busy, especially in summer months. Beware of the canoeists; many of them could be novices who are unable to spot swimmers. Use a tow float and a bright hat to ensure you are clearly visible.

⚠2 Look out for large boulders at the start of the swim.

⚠3 Small, fast-flowing rapids 2k into your swim, ensure you keep right.

⚠4 Fast rapids. Exciting but dangerous, stop and assess before attempting. Keep right to carry on and keep left to exit at Lower Lydbrook. Mind the overhanging branches.

Exit at Lower Lydbrook

KEY

⭐ Swim Entrance/Exit
🅿 Parking
👪 Family friendly
〰 Fast-flowing water
🐟 Salmon Pools
🎣 Fishing
⛱ Picnic Area
🌊 Shallow Water
♿ Accessible
🏊 Family Splash
--- Indicates walk

This is a point-to-point swim section so you will need to leave a car at Lydbrook.

YHA

SHALLOW RAPIDS

LOWER LYDBROOK

Fee for parking

WILD SWIMMER'S VIEWPOINT

We parked, changed and plopped ourselves into the water at Kerne Bridge Canoe Launch, making the start of the swim gentle and easy. During the swim we were able to enjoy quiet spells of mindful swimming, noticing light, movement and colour around. It is a wildlife delight! There was adventure too with the rapids along the way and also at our destination. Water shoes are helpful as the river bed is stony with quite a rush of calf height water at the exit, which was surprisingly difficult to negotiate. We had a vehicle at Lower Lydbrook so didn't have to walk back – that would've been an added adventure!

SECTION: 10	DISTANCE	TIME	GRADE	ACTIVITY
KERNE BRIDGE TO LOWER LYDBROOK	4k (2.6 miles)	45 mins +	▨ ▨	🏊 👪 ♿ 🏊

START POSTCODE: **HR5 9QX** (Kerne Bridge Canoe Launch)   FINISH POSTCODE: **GL17 9NP** (Lower Lydbrook)

MAPS ARE NOT TO SCALE, FOR ROUTE GUIDANCE ONLY

This is not a section for beginners, technical sections

Welsh Bicknor swim start from YHA and St Margaret's Church.

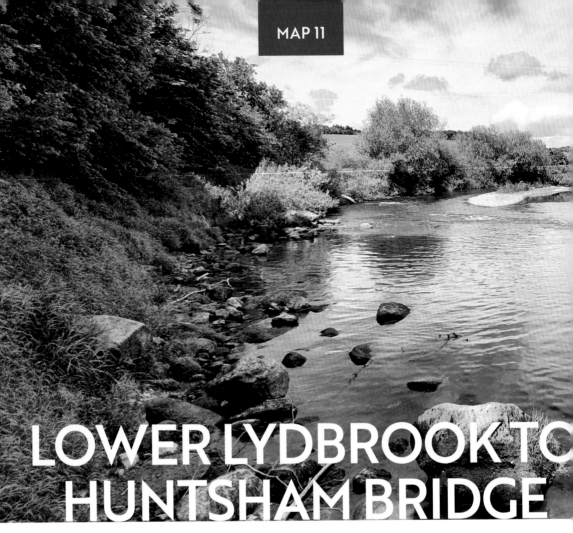

MAP 11

LOWER LYDBROOK TO HUNTSHAM BRIDGE

This is one of the most beautiful sections of the Wye and one of my favourites. Entering the water at Lower Lydbrook it's a short swim downstream to the Youth Hostel and picturesque St Margaret's Church at Welsh Bicknor (this is not in Wales as its name would lead you to believe).

Swimming under the Stowfield Viaduct (Lydbrook, 1875) avoid gettlng too close to the pillars as you swim through! The railway closed in 1964 and this is now a footbridge. You swim some beautiful sections through the Wye Valley before passing under the world-famous viewpoint of Symonds Yat Rock, which towers metres above the River Wye. The river meanders and approaches another limestone area which forms vertical cliffs called Coldwell Rocks: these are home to the Peregrine Falcons that first arrived to nest in the area in 1982 and

Image: M. Flight

the sound of their screech is mesmerisingly eerie as it echoes off the cliff. Another set of shallow, fast rapids then you will swim towards the green iron Huntsham Bridge (1885, restored 1980). Before the bridge, on the right, is a large beach area: you need to exit here and take the footpath back to the road or walk back along the Wye Valley Walk.

Image: M. Cray

Peregrine Falcons may be seen at Symonds Yat Rock

Image: A Jones

View from Yat Rock towards Coppett Hill

ANGELA'S GUIDE

One of my favourite sections - it's like paradise on the Wye!
Park at Lower Lydbrook (fee) and use steps to enter the water.
Head over to the right side of the river, avoiding the large stones
underwater. Keep right for the deepest swim area. 400 metres
on your right you'll pass Welsh Bicknor Youth Hostel, then pass
under Stowfield Viaduct at Lydbrook (be careful of the debris
around pillars). Beautiful deep salmon pools and plenty of
wildlife along the route but watch out for overhanging branches
and a few fast shallow sections that will need you to otter (feet
first, hips high). There are plenty of exits and entry points on
route, but permission is needed as most is private land. You can
either walk back along Wye Valley Walk or get picked up (there's
no parking at Huntsham Bridge). The walk back is spectacular,
parallel to the river and taking you past the world-famous
Symonds Yat Rock. You cross over the Stowfield Viaduct at
Lydbrook and walk to the car park (walk back 8k).

OPEN WATER SWIMMER'S VIEW

Superb spot to drop into the
water, except you have to
walk some way to find the
depth to swim, so suggest
wearing water shoes to make
your life easier. Once in, the
water level means much
sculling, feet first until you
drift into the salmon pools,
where the depth and feel
of the water is exceptional!
It's so stilling and if you're
enjoying your surroundings,
being in Nature and the
moment, then this one ticks
all the boxes!

Angela swimming past Stowfield Viaduct, Lydbrook

Image: I. McCallum

Image: S.Pearce

Strong currents at Lower Lydbrook. Filming with ITV and Sean Fletcher on our beautiful Wye

Image: I. McCallum

Large boulders so sighting is a must!

Image: I. Macdonald

Roe Deer startled by the camera

MAP 11 · LOWER LYDBROOK TO HUNTSHAM BRIDGE

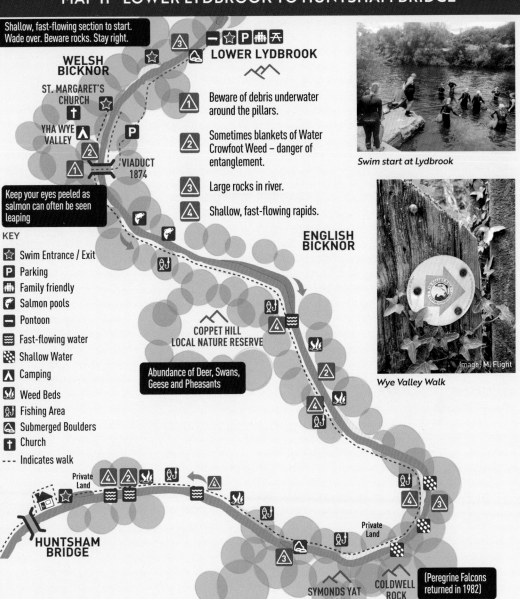

Shallow, fast-flowing section to start. Wade over. Beware rocks. Stay right.

WELSH BICKNOR

ST. MARGARET'S CHURCH

YHA WYE VALLEY

VIADUCT 1874

Keep your eyes peeled as salmon can often be seen leaping

LOWER LYDBROOK

Beware of debris underwater around the pillars.

Sometimes blankets of Water Crowfoot Weed – danger of entanglement.

Large rocks in river.

Shallow, fast-flowing rapids.

ENGLISH BICKNOR

COPPET HILL LOCAL NATURE RESERVE

Abundance of Deer, Swans, Geese and Pheasants

Swim start at Lydbrook

Wye Valley Walk

Image: M. Flight

Private Land

Private Land

HUNTSHAM BRIDGE

SYMONDS YAT ROCK

COLDWELL ROCK

(Peregrine Falcons returned in 1982)

KEY
- ☆ Swim Entrance / Exit
- P Parking
- 🏫 Family friendly
- 🐟 Salmon pools
- — Pontoon
- 🌊 Fast-flowing water
- 🌊 Shallow Water
- ⛺ Camping
- 🌿 Weed Beds
- 🎣 Fishing Area
- ⛰ Submerged Boulders
- ✝ Church
- --- Indicates walk

SECTION: 11	DISTANCE	TIME	GRADE	ACTIVITY
LOWER LYDBROOK TO HUNTSHAM BRIDGE	6.5K (4.03 MILES)	1 HOUR 30 +		

START POSTCODE: GL17 9NP (Lower Lydbrook)   **FINISH POSTCODE: HR9 6JN** (Huntsham Bridge, Goodrich)*

* Private land, seek permission to exit

MAPS ARE NOT TO SCALE, FOR ROUTE GUIDANCE ONLY

Taking the Wye Valley Walk to Lydbrook to swim back down.

Image: I. McCallum

Symonds Yat Rock viewpoint

Image: M.Flight

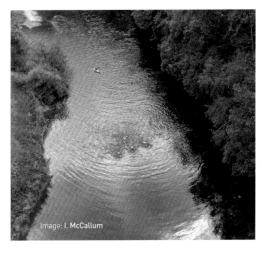

Image: I. McCallum

Lower Lydbrook start section with island and fast flowing water

Swim downstream below Coldwell Rocks

Angela swimming from Lydbrook to Symonds Yat coming up to Huntsham Bridge Image: I. McCallum

MAP 12

HUNTSHAM BRIDGE TO SYMONDS YAT EAST

The swim from Huntsham Bridge to Symonds Yat East is one of the most popular sections of the River Wye, busy with paddlers throughout the year. It takes you through tree-covered cliffs and attractive woodland-wrapped hillsides.

Much of the land surrounding this area is private, so please ensure you seek permission before entering the water here. There is a beach area just above the bridge, which is accessed via a public footpath that leads you into the field, crossing behind the garden of the white house on the bank just before the bridge. Starting your swim, shortly after the bridge you will come to shallow, fast rapids.

As the water becomes deeper, you'll spot the next landmark of St Dubricius Church on your right-hand side, which signifies the approach to Symonds Yat West. Swimming downstream, through a series of deep salmon pools, you will pass a large campsite on your right-hand side and where two river cruise boats are operational. Be aware of boats and strong currents in this area. This part of

river is very popular with fishermen so look out for lines in the water and pass carefully. You will then pass a small (private) beach on your right-hand side, immediately opposite some large rocks in the water. At this point, you are only 350m from Ye Old Ferrie Inn on the right-hand side; this is the oldest and most scenic pub on the Wye. The first of two traditional hand-ferries operates from here. The second is 500 metres downstream at The Saracen's Head, just above the famous grade 2 rapids. EXIT AT THE HAND FERRY either side (permission needed) as it is too dangerous to swim any further! Most access to the River Wye at Symonds West and East is private and permission is needed. One of my bases is Ye Old Ferrie Inn, which serves delicious food with a big welcome. I take regular guided and technique swims from here all year round. The owner, Jamie Hicks, happily welcomes swimmers on the condition you use the pub for food and drink. The Old Court Hotel (owners Tori and Jono) is another of my bases, in a prime location 200 metres from the River Wye and a perfect place to eat and stay. The Hotel dates back 450 years and is set in stunning gardens.

Swim event in Symonds Yat West led by Swim Wild Wye

Angela in her office at Ye Olde Ferrie Inn

Hand Ferry, Saracen's Head

MAP 12 · HUNTSHAM BRIDGE TO SYMONDS YAT EAST

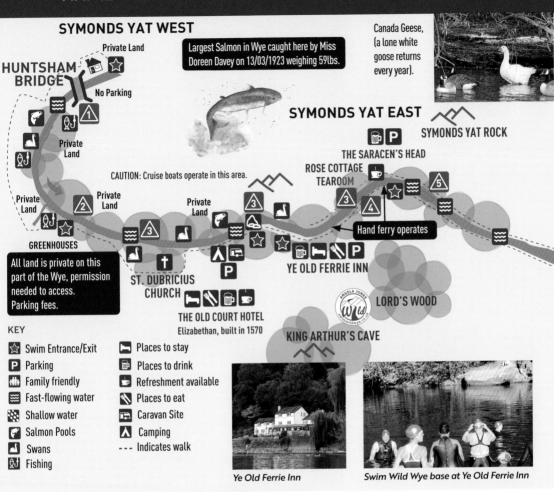

SYMONDS YAT WEST

Private Land

HUNTSHAM BRIDGE

No Parking

Private Land

Largest Salmon in Wye caught here by Miss Doreen Davey on 13/03/1923 weighing 59lbs.

Canada Geese, (a lone white goose returns every year).

SYMONDS YAT EAST

SYMONDS YAT ROCK

THE SARACEN'S HEAD

ROSE COTTAGE TEAROOM

CAUTION: Cruise boats operate in this area.

Private Land

Private Land

Private Land

Private Land

Hand ferry operates

GREENHOUSES

All land is private on this part of the Wye, permission needed to access. Parking fees.

ST. DUBRICIUS CHURCH

YE OLD FERRIE INN

LORD'S WOOD

THE OLD COURT HOTEL
Elizabethan, built in 1570

KING ARTHUR'S CAVE

KEY

- ⭐ Swim Entrance/Exit
- 🅿 Parking
- 👪 Family friendly
- 〰 Fast-flowing water
- ▨ Shallow water
- 🐟 Salmon Pools
- 🦢 Swans
- 🎣 Fishing
- 🛏 Places to stay
- 🍺 Places to drink
- 🍺 Refreshment available
- 🍴 Places to eat
- 🚐 Caravan Site
- ⛺ Camping
- --- Indicates walk

Ye Old Ferrie Inn

Swim Wild Wye base at Ye Old Ferrie Inn

⚠ Shallow, fast rapids at the start.

⚠ Navigational section which gets busy in summer months, ensure you are visible with tow floats and bright hats. Look out for other water users.

⚠ Beware of river cruise boats.

⚠ Busiest section of the Wye.

⚠ Fast rapids – DO NOT SWIM.

SECTION: 12	DISTANCE	TIME	GRADE	ACTIVITY
HUNTSHAM BRIDGE TO YE OLD FERRIE INN	3K (2.48 MILES)	40 mins +		🏊
GREENHOUSES TO YE OLD FERRIE INN	2K (1.24 MILES)	25 mins+		🏊
YE OLD FERRIE INN TO SARACEN'S HEAD	1K (0.62 MILES)	10 mins		🏊
START POSTCODE: **HR9 6JN** (Huntsham Bridge) FINISH POSTCODE: **HR9 6JL** (Saracen's Head)				

MAPS ARE NOT TO SCALE, FOR ROUTE GUIDANCE ONLY

One of the many swim entrances along this section

The Old Court Hotel, a 14th century coach house

A walk along this lovely stretch of riverbank to start point

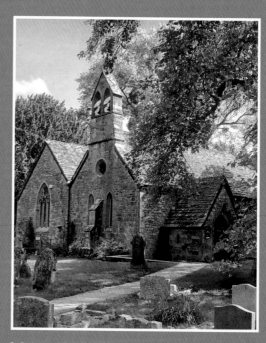

St Dubricius Church, 12th century

Swim Wild Wye guided swim Huntsham Bridge

Image: I. McCallum

MAP 13

Image: I. McCallum, Biblins Bridge

BIBLINS TO MONMOUTH

This magical swim crosses the borders, starting in England and finishing in Wales. Biblins Bridge is a spectacular rope footbridge originally built in 1957: it provides pedestrian access from the west side of the river to the east side at Symonds Yat. The bridge was heavily damaged during the Storm Dennis floods in February 2020 and was repaired and reopened.

There are amazing views of the Wye Valley, the River Wye and the Doward from the bridge. The swim entrance side is private and owned by the Forestry Commission, so please request permission to swim from here. As you leave Biblins and make your way downstream you will encounter the Seven Sisters Rocks on the right-hand side, there are also caves on this side of the river such as the limestone King Arthur's Cave situated in King's Wood. Meandering downstream the overhanging trees lining the banks of the river here are extremely dense; the river widens in sections to provide some lovely deep swim areas. Hadnock Islands are located in the centre of the river, about 2km downstream. This fast and often furious flowing section is best navigated on the left-hand side. For the next few kilometres, you'll encounter some deep salmon pools with the odd cormorant drying itself on one of the many embedded branches on the riverbed, so stay alert to debris! A large beach on the

Monmouth Rowing Club exit by Wye Bridge

right-hand side, with a high bank, marks the 2k distance to Monmouth and offers a possible early exit point with the Wye Valley Walk running parallel all the way to Monmouth. From here to Monmouth is a busy rowing section, so sighting is a must! 1k further downstream you will see St Peter's Church at Dixton, on the right-hand side, this marks the 1k distance to Monmouth. There is a pontoon just after the church where you could early exit if needed. Arriving at Monmouth you need to exit the river at second set of steps, on the right-hand side, before the Wye Bridge.

ANGELA'S THOUGHTS

You will need to walk up from Monmouth Rowing Club 7km to enter the river from the concrete pontoon at Biblins Woodcraft Centre (permission needed). You will quickly enter a fast-flowing section. Ottering may be needed, depending on the water levels. 2k into the swim you will reach Hadnock Islands; at this point you will need to assess and pass either side of the island. The left side is usually less obstructed by weeds. Strong undercurrents and eddies are often found in this section. The rock formations surrounding this area are second to none, however, the technical side of the swim doesn't allow for much sight-seeing. Meandering down to Monmouth on the remainder of this route allows for the final 2k to be enjoyed without too much technical surveying but be warned, if you aren't alert then you are likely to come into contact with a rowing boat or a paddle board!

2k swim downstream to Monmouth

Beach at 2k start, Monmouth

Rowers at Monmouth

The pontoon at the 1k mark from St Peter's Church, Monmouth

Swim Wild Wye group walk up to start at Biblins

MAP 13 · BIBLINS TO MONMOUTH

SEVEN SISTERS ROCK

BIBLINS

1mile downstream Hadnock Islands. Fast-flowing water with strong undercurrents, debris and heavy weed.

HADNOCK ISLAND

St Peter's Church, Dixton (12th century) 1k from Monmouth

△1 Navigational river with two rowing clubs operating in this area. Keep sighting and ensure you are highly visible (tow float and bright hat).

△2 Committed swim section as there are no exit points before the 2k and 1k point to Monmouth.

△3 Strong currents around Hadnock Island

Hadnock Island

The distance options on this swim follow the annual Great Wye Swim - inclusive to all.

MONMOUTH GREAT WYE SWIM Wild

WYE VALLEY WALK

Beach area 2k from Monmouth is an ideal family area and 2k swim down.

Pontoon 1k from Monmouth provides an ideal beginner / short swim distance

ST. PETER'S CHURCH

Monmouth swim exit at second steps

KEY

- ☆ Swim Entrance/Exit
- Ⓟ Parking
- 👪 Family friendly
- ≋ Fast-flowing water
- 🌲 Rowing Club
- ▬ Pontoon
- 🔳 Shallow Water
- 🌿 Weed Beds
- 🎣 Fishing
- 🏛 Places to visit
- 🏕 Places to stay
- 🔪 Places to eat
- ☕ Places to drink
- --- Indicates walk

MONMOUTH ROWING CLUB CAR PARK

Private Land

Private Land

WYE BRIDGE

MONMOUTH

SECTION: 13	DISTANCE	TIME	GRADE	ACTIVITY
BIBLINS TO MONMOUTH	9K (5.6 MILES)	1.30 hours +	■	🏊
MONMOUTH BEACH TO WYE BRIDGE	2K (1.24 MILES)	20mins +	■	🏊 🤿 👪
PONTOON TO WYE BRIDGE	1K (0.62 MILES)	10 mins+	■	🏊 🤿 👪
START POSTCODE: HR9 6DX (Biblins Woodcraft) FINISH POSTCODE: NP25 3DP (Monmouth Rowing Club)				

Hadnock Island

This is not a lake or the sea.
This is the Wye.
Diverse, technical and forever
changing.
Angela Jones

Image: I. McCattum

Monmouth Viaduct, River Wye, near Monmouth. This disused railway viaduct once carried the line from Monmouth to Tintern and into the Forest of Dean. Fast flowing, shallow rapids

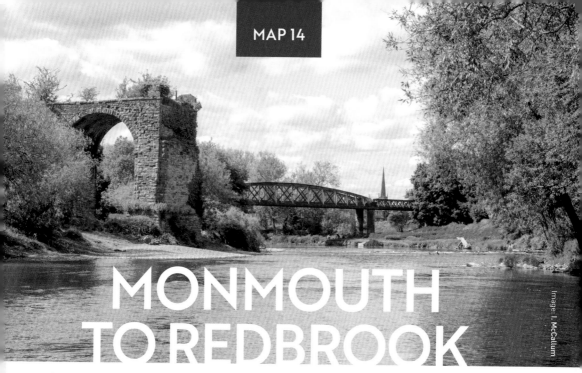

MAP 14

Image: I. McCallum

MONMOUTH TO REDBROOK

My final swim section is Monmouth to Redbrook which provides another opportunity to travel along the Wales/England border. This is the final stretch of the Wye I recommend swimming as past Redbrook it becomes tidal and is too dangerous to swim.

Entering the water at Monmouth, look up towards the hill in front and you'll spot the Kymin Round House and an 18th century Naval Temple. From the second set of steps at Monmouth Rowing Club you'll swim under Wye Bridge almost immediately encountering small, fast flowing rapids after the bridge. Stay to the left-hand side at this point. If you prefer to avoid swimming under the bridge and through the current, there is a second entrance option from a beach 200 metres on the left-hand side past the Wye Bridge. Meandering downstream you'll swim under an iron bridge (Duke of Beaufort Bridge) that crosses the river and just after this the river Monnow joins the Wye.

Monmouth Viaduct, a derelict stone railway bridge, appears shortly after, on your right-hand side. You'll immediately be in shallow, fast rapids for a few hundred metres! Ottering is essential feet first, hips high. As you swim through the majestic Wye Valley, the river opens out to provide some lovely swim stretches and you are surrounded by beautiful woodland. As the lovely English village of Redbrook comes into sight, there is a series of large boulders in the water, just before you reach the village. Your swim will finish at a small shingle beach on the left-hand side, directly after the iron bridge that links Redbrook with Penallt, which you will swim under.

Rough waters. A tough technical swim down to Redbrook

Wye Bridge, Monmouth

Kayakers negotiate one of the 5 pillars, Wye Bridge (1615)

Egrets are becoming more frequent visitors to the Wye

Angela exiting at Redbrook

MAP 14 · MONMOUTH TO REDBROOK

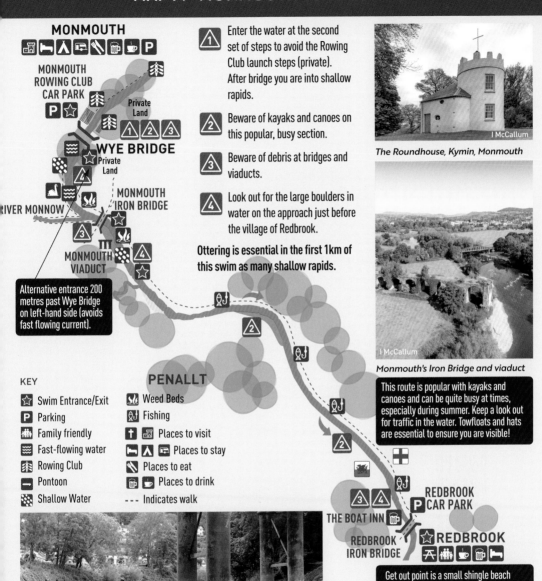

MONMOUTH

MONMOUTH ROWING CLUB CAR PARK

Private Land

WYE BRIDGE

Private Land

RIVER MONNOW

MONMOUTH IRON BRIDGE

MONMOUTH VIADUCT

Alternative entrance 200 metres past Wye Bridge on left-hand side (avoids fast flowing current).

1 Enter the water at the second set of steps to avoid the Rowing Club launch steps (private). After bridge you are into shallow rapids.

2 Beware of kayaks and canoes on this popular, busy section.

3 Beware of debris at bridges and viaducts.

4 Look out for the large boulders in water on the approach just before the village of Redbrook.

Ottering is essential in the first 1km of this swim as many shallow rapids.

The Roundhouse, Kymin, Monmouth
I McCallum

Monmouth's Iron Bridge and viaduct
I McCallum

PENALLT

KEY

⭐	Swim Entrance/Exit	🌊	Weed Beds
🅿	Parking	🎣	Fishing
👪	Family friendly	🏕	Places to visit
≋	Fast-flowing water	🏠	Places to stay
🌲	Rowing Club	🍴	Places to eat
▬	Pontoon	🍺☕	Places to drink
▨	Shallow Water	---	Indicates walk

This route is popular with kayaks and canoes and can be quite busy at times, especially during summer. Keep a look out for traffic in the water. Towfloats and hats are essential to ensure you are visible!

REDBROOK CAR PARK

THE BOAT INN

REDBROOK IRON BRIDGE

REDBROOK

Get out point is a small shingle beach with stone steps on left-hand side directly after the iron viaduct (Penallt Viaduct) which crosses the river

Redbrook Iron Bridge

SECTION: 14	DISTANCE	TIME	GRADE	ACTIVITY
MONMOUTH TO REDBROOK	4.8k (2.9 miles)	1 hour +		🏊

START POSTCODE: **NP25 3DP** (Monmouth Rowing Club) FINISH POSTCODE: **NP25 4LR** (Redbrook Play Park)

MAPS ARE NOT TO SCALE, FOR ROUTE GUIDANCE ONLY

Redbrook Iron Bridge, our final destination on our swim journey of the Wye.

Sharing Nocturnal Nature

Barn Owl - M. Cray

Rare Bechstein's Bat - S. Wadley

Badger – I. MacDonald

SwimWildWye guided night swim

Angela sleeping on magical riverbank in bivy bag.

Angela bathes in the moonlight.

Night Swimming

Night swimming offers the unbridled privilege of sharing the watery space with nocturnal Nature. It sharpens your senses and makes your soul soar. Discover a wild world that is not often seen, but which is a definite favourite of mine. I often combine a night swim with wild camping on the river's edge, where Nature puts on such a special show.

Minnows flicker and jump in the moonlight and the beautiful Wye bats dip and dart over the river as they hunt for food. Often, I will see the fantastic Mr Fox glide by, sometimes making a pheasant screech in protest at being disturbed. Muntjac deer bark deep in the forest, a distinctive 'plop' gives away an otter's otherwise slick entry into the river, and Roe deer venture to the river's edge for an unhurried drink.

Far from provoking fear, the dark provides another magical show from Nature - and it is an absolute privilege to be in the audience.

My Swim Story
Outdoor Swimmer Article, March 2018

MY SWIM STORY

The River Wye

51-year-old Angela Jones spent five weeks exploring her favourite river, the Wye

I have swum all over the world and the UK but there is only one place that holds me... The Wye. It runs through my veins and is my workplace and playground. Early last August I set off for 5 weeks with my dog Jack to explore the whole of the Wye. Kayaking it first, running back up it and then swimming down it. Starting from the source in the Cambrian Mountains, I slept on its banks as I continued my journey. I kayaked 100 miles, ran 160 miles and swam 84 miles.

Jack was the first dog to take part in the Bog Snorkelling Champs

AT HOME ON THE RIVER

I can be found swimming the Wye all year round. And more often than not, gliding along the river beds, where the excitement of a glimpse of eels and fish in weeds is truly magical. I always felt more at home in and under the river than on land. Mono fins are a favourite of mine as I can shoot along the river bed and see much more.

The swim took about nine days. For the whole five weeks away, I had no real focus on anything but playing on the Wye. I shot rapids and felt its force; I also saw its calm, serene state. Some sections I glided down, some I was catapulted down. At every opportunity I deep pool dived and bounced along the glorious depths.

I tasted the sweet clear water and the pollution of the busy Hereford section. I even managed to pop over to the World Bog Snorkelling Championships and take part with my dog. One night I slept out at Gilfach nature reserve and swam in the ice falls and deep pools looking at rock formations.

I KAYAKED 100 MILES, RAN 160 MILES AND SWAM 84 MILES

ECSTASY

I got slapped by a huge salmon that I surprised, glided over eels in the weeds, watched cormorants diving. I had the excitement of a child. I slept out on the banks and shared the pleasure of sleeping and waking on its banks for five ecstatic weeks.

Angela introduces people to the beauty of the river Wye with her adventure business run-wild.co.uk

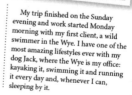

My trip finished on the Sunday evening and work started Monday morning with my first client, a wild swimmer in the Wye. I have one of the most amazing lifestyles ever with my dog Jack, where the Wye is my office: kayaking it, swimming it and running it every day and, whenever I can, sleeping by it.

What's your Swim Story? Email: editor@outdoorswimmer.com